Cont€

Acknowledgements

Thanks to Chris Charlesworth and Andy Neill at Omnibus Press.

Guy Garvey, Mark Potter, Craig Potter, Pete Turner, Richard Jupp, John Bramwell and the great I Am Kloot, Guy Lovelady and Ugly Man, one of Manchester's mightiest labels, Andy Rourke, John Nuttall, Todd Eckhart, Chris Hewitt and Ozit Morpheus, Tony Michaelides, Michael Mackey, Dave Haslam, Sue Langford, Simon Donahue, Barney Hoskyns, Terry Christian, Mark Radcliffe, Dermo Northside, Clint Boon, Phil Chadwick, Michael Winterbottom, Chris Coupe, George Borowski, Henry Normal, Doves, Pete Jobson, Blueprint Studios, John Robb, Simon Reynolds, Tim and Maxi Hudson, Joe Matera, Luke Turner, Sean McGhee, Julia Adamson, Gary Atkinson, CP and Pam Lee, Mark Hodkinson, Ro and John Barrat.

Special thanks to: Lindsay Reade, Tosh Ryan, Kathryn Turner, Karen Middlehurst, Julie Howard and Katrina and Ben Cross of Bribie Island and all at the *Warrington Guardian*.

Sources: BBC 6 Music, *The Bury Times*, *Clash*, *Classic Rock*, *The Daily Telegraph*, Granada Television, *The Guardian*, *The Independent*, The Manchester Busker, *Manchester Evening News*, Manchester Festival, *MOJO*, *Panache*, *Q*, *The Quietus*, *Record Collector*, *The Rochdale Observer*, *Rock'n'Reel*, Rock's Back Pages, *Subculture Manchester*, *The Times* and Unconvention/Blueprint Studios.

Introduction

It's now mid-2009 and Elbow stand at the crossroads. Almost two decades of history lies in their wake. Eighteen years of being in the shadows; four albums, several hundred gigs, several million whispers, the friendly voice of anti-celebrity. For so long they had remained the secret of some kind of underground; a hidden beauty and a dark enigma, sumptuous and ever-so-slightly illicit.

How things have changed. The band's hugely celebrated triumph of 2008 has hurtled them towards a giant audience, with one song in particular, 'One Day Like This', seeping from the walls that guarded that secret, on to radio and television, soundtracking documentary and sports shows alike. Elbow have finally received the attention they always deserved and seemed destined never to find.

But who are the invisible masses who purchased Elbow's Mercury Prize, Brit Award winning *The Seldom Seen Kid*? I have an intelligent, articulate friend who has listened attentively to all of Elbow's albums, has watched them at a variety of mud-splattered English festivals and yet still, somehow, doesn't get it.

"I can't grasp what is special here," she admitted, just a week ago.

"How do you know when you are an Elbow fan?"

Not a bad question, actually. There is no question of genre here. You don't belong to any known club. Despite Elbow's comparatively advanced years, it doesn't appear to be an age thing at all.

"When did you first get Elbow?" she enquired.

My mind flashed back to sparsely attended gigs in darkened cellars on Manchester's Oldham Street. Although I had seen the comparatively youthful band on a small number of occasions at gigs in the city's Northern Quarter, I hadn't quite connected with them, despite the fact I was a long-term admirer of some of the people closest to them – John Bramwell, I Am Kloot and Doves among others. It took something precise, different and utterly personal to find myself in a position to be touched by Elbow.

It was my birthday. It was painful. I was out and I was arguing. Arguing with a woman I loved who had, it seemed, 'moved on'.

Suffice it to say, the evening didn't end well. I arrived home with a bunch of birthday presents, finding myself drifting into that surreal state of heartbreak. One of these presents happened to be Elbow's first album, the reflective, forceful, poetic beauty titled *Asleep In The Back*. It somehow seemed such an unlikely present and Elbow, I truly thought, had seen their moment wither and die. But there was something special there.

I played it twice through on the hop. It wasn't the standard 'break-up', album and, like some, I always had Dylan's *Blood On The Tracks* on standby, just in case things went badly wrong. It wasn't remotely twee or hugely self-indulgent either. Nor did it seem maudlin. There was something almost joyful about a lyric that began in a dark place and twisted into a barrage of surreal imagery – uplifting imagery.

I only vaguely knew who singer Guy Garvey was as his Bury roots didn't exactly shine through. But I loved the way that Elbow seemed wholly unafraid to use pre-punk influences; Pink Floyd most obviously, but I heard all kinds of bands that might appear unhip – there was even a touch of ELO in there. By the end of the second play-through, I was smiling while sinking the Merlot. Elbow were already a special band.

I was a fan. It was an inner thing. I had sat down that night, thoroughly expecting another chunk of dross aiming for indie-landfill. I was wrong. In time Elbow would become – Radiohead fans stay calm

– the greatest British band of their time. If you had told me this at the time, I wouldn't have been surprised.

The basic notion behind this book stretches back several years. At the time, the subject wasn't to be centred solely on Elbow and, in fact, came with a different and self-explanatory title: *'Pounding' Doves, I Am Kloot, Elbow and the Sound of the Manchester Underground.* It was in that order of eminence too, with Elbow, rock's perennial underachievers, most definitely Manchester's best kept secret. There are echoes of that lost and never-to-be-written book here.

For so many years, this was the position inhabited by Elbow. When trying to convey frustration whenever some shallow new pop sensation would grasp the media spotlight, I thought, "What about bloody Elbow? They have no chance, this day and age."

Elbow are a triumph of heart over empty style, of emotion over the superficial, of reality over celebrity. They are a reactionary band in the sense that they have retreated to the days when musicality was good and image was of secondary importance. For Elbow are nothing if not multi-dimensional. Funk boys and indie scallywags one minute, heartfelt soul boys and shameless proggers the next. This is the most obvious reason why Elbow are loved, for they represent the best of all the great music that has permeated our lives over the years. Good taste in short.

That alone would be enough. But there is a rare honesty here; reportage, if you like, of everyday life. Garvey's celebrated lyricism is, at once, childish and bristling with intelligence. It speaks a simplistic language and, by tradition, it has no place at the front of such sophisticated music. When, post-Mercury Awards, Elbow performed with a full orchestra, the lyrics occasionally seemed ill-fitting. This is a now time-honoured Garvey trick – the paradox of beautiful orchestration underlying outbursts of everyday Northern angst. After a while, after several listens, what seems awkward suddenly seems perfectly natural. That's a vision of an artist in the true sense of the word.

It's exactly what Guy Garvey is – in a similar way to Morrissey or Mark E. Smith. However, there lies another difference for Garvey, by many accounts, is wholly approachable, not the celebrated curmudgeon as in Smith or the wholly aloof Morrissey. He is often to be seen wandering along Manchester's Oxford Road, frequenting a number of local bars, often standing alone and perfectly willing to chat to anyone who happens by. Yet this affable giant of a man is also known for not answering text messages, not replying to phone calls, not returning communication. A naturally reticent man, whose shyness informs his music. As with all shy people, it's easy to misunderstand, to under-rate, and to dismiss, one reason why so many years passed without Elbow making any serious headway.

However, when the message finally emerged to a large market, it was all the more powerful for its time in the shadows. It is, therefore, the true sound of the underground.

Chapter One

Bury and Bryan

The heart of Lancashire, the hub of the industrial revolution, is surrounded by evocative Cottonopolis. The names of the towns close by – Preston, Burnley, Rochdale, Wigan, Oldham, Blackburn – resonate with images of cultural clichés; the dark Satanic rows of red brick terraces, sprawling markets, hearts of gold and grit. The evocative northern imagery still exists and, without doubt, in all the Lancashire towns, there still exist elements of day-to-day strife. But there is also considerable regeneration. The Pennine–Lancashire dream, inspired, in part, by Tony Wilson and logoed by Peter Saville, has seen the area shift to a new contemporary level, as far from Lowry-esque landscapes as it is possible to get.

Despite this, Bury is slightly closer to Manchester than the other towns, its true cultural neighbour being the Salford of Prestwich, Cheetham Hill, Sedgley Park, Heaton Park, all languishing significantly on the other side of the M60 ring road. Bury is indicative of the north Manchester psyche. In musical terms, this is important. Think of Mark E. Smith and his lifelong home of Prestwich, his band, The Fall, a Salfordian dream, a north Manchester attitude against Factory Records with its sharp sleeves and contrived images.

"We couldn't ever have signed for Factory ... southern Manchester trendies ... we are fro 'up here'"

"Up here" evoking the aloofness of satellite towns. Nowhere is this more epitomised than Bury. More relevant is the fact that Smith's iconic 'diamond' knotted jumper of 1979 had been purchased by his mother from Bury's famous market. A jumper from Bury market could be seen as the ultimate riposte to the lavishly garbed new romantic creatures of London's Camden.

In Smith's florid lyricism, Bury was symbolic in the sense that, in his eyes, it was a town of grounded intelligence as opposed to Stockport's shiny car pretensions. Equally interesting was Bury's Square One Studios. Back in the mid Eighties, this pristine rectangular studio provided a north Manchester alternative to Stockport's Strawberry Studios, which had been producing high quality Manchester recordings since the late Sixties. Typically of Bury, Square One seemed a deliberately businesslike, pedantic studio, bereft of the cosy glamour of Strawberry, which had been built from the base of the 10cc/Mindbenders musician clique.

In the mid Eighties, north Manchester bands such as The Chameleons and The Monkey Run produced recordings of comparable sheen from the Bury studio.

But back then songwriting seemed a lost and archaic art. The very idea of a rock band or a singer-songwriter evening would be the subject of hip youthful mockery. "Guitars are for dads. Singer-songwriters? Do me a favour." And yet Elbow, who would emerge into the mainstream some two decades down the line, were firmly rooted in such an esteemed tradition. Equally bizarre, the band most closely associated with Elbow, if only for their age, geographical location and facial hair, were Doves – a band firmly rooted not in the singer-songwriter genre but on the Hacienda dancefloor and, in their previous incarnation as Sub-Sub, scoring chart success during the age of 'Madchester'.

Crafted songwriting was not for the hedonists of distinction, who crammed the postulating vibe of the Hacienda. The media came to Manchester to witness an orgy of dance, of beer-bellied men in orange T-shirts, girls spinning around the edge of the dance floor, the idiotic worship of the DJ, the imported sounds of the E generation.

That's not to knock it too much – the movement was a release of energy, a "flash", if one was to take music journalist Simon Reynolds' line, that pushed music to a new level and certainly pushed Manchester to a new level, pumping youth and vibrancy into the city's ongoing regeneration plan. In the wake of Happy Mondays, the shape-shifting local bands suddenly pushed the rhythm, becoming both danceable and bankable. Even James, one-time purveyors of weird folk, were transformed into an awkwardly effective semi-dance act and, in their wake, The Mock Turtles, spinning from sullen indie to enter the realms of the new psychedelia, as well as a host of others, from World Of Twist to Northside.

The media camped on Whitworth Street, filtering the message across the world. Manchester had become a home of dance and ecstasy, garbed in Gio Goi, the streetwise threads of Happy Mondays, supplied by brilliant chancers the Bagianno brothers. In the city centre it sure was kicking off, but slowly turning from Day-Glo to darkness.

While the Hacienda captured headlines, at the other end of Whitworth Street, within the railway arch named The Green Room, emerged a wholly different and individual artistic upsurge, seemingly unloved, profoundly unhip and unhyped, apart from in the local press. An event called The Manchester Busker started to silently gather pace. It was simple in format and, I proudly state, partly insti-gated by the author, who deserves none of the credit, which is all due to the tireless work of promoter Chris Coupe and business partner Damian Brehony, together known as CC Brickwall.

Mocked by those seemingly in the know, these singer-songwriters, comedians and ranting poets, by a painfully slow process, started to build their own audience. From this lost breed came a rich seam of tal-ent – filtering out from Caroline Aherne's initial success as Sister Mary Immaculate and Mrs Merton, who began life as a Frank Sidebottom character. Beyond that came Steve Coogan and Henry Normal, his partner in Baby Cow Productions, rising from being a lonely, penniless poet living in the darkened rooms of Failsworth sending off demo tapes to local papers, to Henry Normal, the unlikely saviour of the British comedy empire, now collector of BAFTAS...

Why is this relevant to a book about Elbow?

Beyond the success of Coogan, Normal, Aherne, Craig Cash et al, were the songwriters who punctuated those Manchester Busker performances, great, royally ignored lost talents who believed wholeheartedly in the power of the song. The small but big-hearted singer-songwriter John Bramwell, known as Johnny Dangerously who, years down the line, would re-emerge to worldwide cultish appeal as the idiosyncratic songwriting force behind I Am Kloot. Through a series of albums filled with disparate songs, filching from every given genre, I Am Kloot slowly evolved into a genuine triumph of unfettered songwriting.

There were others. Perennial Manchester 'outsider' songwriter George Borowski, previously known as 'Guitar George' and still, as I write, releasing great and ignored albums, lost classics. And, of course, the late Bryan Glancy, now known as the muse behind Elbow, the man to whom the band dedicated their Mercury Prize.

A gentle soul locked in an unlikely place where The Velvet Underground might meet Neil Young ... and in that class, too. A lost, legendary, shadowy figure in shades, self-effacing, darkly, unfashionably 'nice', popping up, mid-set, to deliver 'Propping Up The Bar', a great little gem among a nest of great little gems.

Bryan was all heart, all vision, all talent – attributes that were largely absent during the days of Happy Mondays. However there was no visible bitterness with Bryan. He became known as a perennial scenester; a big-hearted ferocious enthusiast, introducing people to people, musicians to musicians, and journalists to journalists, not for his own gain.

At the turn of the Nineties, Glancy and Dangerously could be seen almost nightly on small pub stages, arts centres and semi-comedy venues of Manchester. It was a world away from the Hacienda's famous thrust, but no less valuable. I recall talking to Bryan at a Busker event at The Romiley Forum in Cheshire.

"What on Earth are we doing playing out here?" he laughed. "It's because you live here, don't you? And you will give us a write-up."

It was and I did. That night, alone on an unlikely stage, Bryan was little short of awesome before a first-time audience comprising parochial strays catching an easy night out. A gathering who, upon entering, had little idea of what a Manchester Busker event might be, an audience not entirely suited to the charms of Johnny Dangerously and Bryan Glancy.

The story of Elbow begins here because, as Guy Garvey would often state, both Johnny and Bryan would become massively important in Elbow's development. Glancy would gain a shadowy omnipresence in the echoes of all four albums to date by Elbow, who would make certain that his name would never be forgotten.

Although Elbow would be forever associated with the songwriting fringes of the Manchester music scene and would garner much fondness for that, things are not always so black and white. In a March 2009 interview with Q magazine, Guy Garvey expressed the view that, without The Stone Roses, Elbow would never have existed. "They left a legacy, the Roses," Garvey stated. "That style of rhythm-wah that John Squire played on that first record is what every 15-year-old lad goes for. Even now. They start with the Roses and move forward."

As a 15-year-old lad Garvey would take the train from Bury into Manchester every weekend. It was a complete look, part encouraged by the hippy style of his sisters, now morphed into the Madchester scene that couldn't help but affect him. It was, as he stated, "like United and City", the choice was simple. Happy Mondays, with their loose funk rave and state of seemingly endless party, or The Stone Roses, fully embracing the dance scene and yet retaining the distance of a proper band. Garvey naturally swung to the latter as he had spent years listening to the late Sixties music that was such a heady influence on the Roses. The Byrds, Joni Mitchell, James Taylor, Neil Young, Crosby, Stills & Nash, Grateful Dead as well as Fairport Convention, John Martyn and Nick Drake.

"... Everybody started dressing like it was a retake on Woodstock," Garvey told *Uncut*. "It was just amazing. It was all right for lads to wear flowers and stuff again. I had a paisley bandana, a pair of massive 16-inch bellbottom jeans and floral hoodies a go-go."

Garvey's Roses fixation came to a head when, following a period of exile, *NME* tracked the band down to Bury's Square One Studios, much to the amazement of Guy himself.

"It was like *Whistle Down The Wind* where she thinks she has found Jesus in a barn. The whole world was looking for them [The Stone Roses] and they were in our hometown."

Funnily enough, future Elbow guitarist Mark Potter was working as a pizza delivery boy in Bury and, to his utter astonishment, found himself delivering to The Stone Roses at Square One. The only problem being that no one in the town would believe him. Not that it mattered. The link had been made. The Stone Roses, already one classic album deep into their own legend, had become little short of gods on the streets of places like Bury. Despite having been rather disliked by the Manchester elite for some years, the Roses had become more than a band – they were a look, an attitude, a grimace, the first truly 'Manc' band. Their studied belligerence would be copied half a decade later with the sudden explosion of Oasis.

There were obvious differences between Elbow and The Stone Roses; Elbow would not become 'style icons', front a new upsurge or movement, marry rock to dance or become synonymous with any kind of serious 'attitude'. Nevertheless, there would be similarities between the early years of both bands. The Stone Roses, it is often forgotten, spent a number of years floundering in an unfashionable obscurity, their glittering talent failing to dent the rather closed shop in their own city; their early rockist leanings – which seem so ironic in retrospect – setting them aside from the house-music-soaked Hacienda elite.

Born 6 March 1974, Guy Edward John Patrick Garvey was named by his mother after Guy Fawkes. If this strikes a revolutionary streak, then it is further backed by the fact that Guy's older brother, Marcus, was named after the Jamaican black nationalist

Marcus Garvey, whose name also featured in numerous reggae lyrics from the mid-Seventies dub period. Surprisingly, his mother had spent time as a policewoman before having to leave the force when she married. Later, her driven determination to make her own way in life would surface when she attended university, *Educating Rita*-style, to gain a psychology degree.

Although not unheard of, even in Bury, switching from running a household to a rather more ambiguous social position as a psychologist was certainly unusual. However, rather like Mark E. Smith and Morrissey, Guy Garvey came from a Lancashire background where working-class values were spiced by intellectualism. The notion that a working-class family from north Manchester would be held by the parameters of the shallow mainstream would not affect the Garvey family. The now, sadly all but lost idea of devouring books for the sake of knowledge and not merely to push through some exam was evident throughout Guy's childhood. By all accounts his schooling was never interrupted by bouts of apathy or raucous behaviour and he never lost faith in the power of literature.

The centrepiece of the family living room was the book-stacked chimney breast, which offered all manner of intriguing tomes. Various encyclopaedias beckoned and would often be used in sturdy consultation to settle a family debate. Fiction and non-fiction were evenly mixed, with the best old-school novels of the mid-20th century such as Alan Sillitoe's *The Loneliness Of The Long Distance Runner* sharing space with political tomes from esteemed commentators like John Pilger and the best American writers such as Norman Mailer, John Updike and Ken Kesey.

The heart of this literary bent probably came from his father, a proofreader who worked the night shift with Mirror Group Newspapers. He was probably more liberal than such a position might suggest.[*] During the early Eighties, his trade union stance took

[*] The Mirror Group was, for better or worse, doused in the stranglehold of trade unionism, ever since transforming from the old Odhams Press in the Sixties and falling under the dark shadow of Robert Maxwell.

him to the picket lines as Thatcher's grip tightened. Riots at Warrington, during the *Stockport Messenger* print workers' battle with Eddie Shah, changed the course of local newspaper production. His support for this was tempered with pangs of guilt as his brother was a policeman. In times of intense polarisation, this would split many families, as Guy Garvey noted in *Q*, "Thatcher turned the police into her foot soldiers – she literally turned brother against brother. My dad never made it personal and if he had been out fighting with coppers, he would never tell us because he wanted us to respect the police. I suppose I get my sense of civic pride and duty from my dad."

Guy's father always brought home both the *Daily Mirror*, with its legacy of the left, and the opposing *Daily Telegraph*, which arguably provided the finest news coverage in the country. It wasn't difficult to pass both tabloid and broadsheet onto the eager Garvey, whose precocious curiosity was evident, according to his elder sister Gina.

"Guy was always soaking things in. Always listening at school. It was obvious he would be an artist of some kind ... or a journalist, perhaps."

Gina was just one of five sisters (along with Samantha, Karen, Louise and Becky) all older than Guy and all with seemingly bohemian tastes in music, clothing and general outlook. Far from the standard Bury household, the prevailing intelligent liberalism could only have had a profound effect. The Garveys' dinner table also proved an unlikely training ground. Gina remembers "regular and lively discussions about politics, social situations and literature".

These discussions openly encouraged Guy's burgeoning intellectualism in a way that didn't excite him at school. He would often use elongated debates to full effect, grasping the limelight and inadvertently shaping his early stagecraft. "The conversations were not always intense," said Gina. "They could also be humorous and very funny. They were 'performances', no doubt about that now."

Gina also revealed that these post-dinner chats could be quite cruel. If Guy embarked on a particularly pretentious tack, his talk would be met with shouts of, "Boring ... shudupppp!"

"It could be cruel at times," admitted Gina.

Such exchanges later helped Garvey to pare down his lyricism, keeping his observations interesting and pertinent for people to utilise within their own experience. His parents' divorce would also prove to be an important factor. Without doubt, Garvey's writing, which had already started to fill numerous notebooks, would become more and more introspective. More private, one might suggest, with the young boy using words to arrest his discomfort.

"I had always been dramatic as a small child," he told The *Guardian* in March 2009. "I remember crying into the mirror when I was about nine or 10 years old. Real amateur dramatics. I am one of seven kids with a big family in a small house, you have got to be dramatic to get noticed."

There were other problems. Crassly, Garvey's 'open-door' ears would cause him to be bullied at school. It was a pathetic physical problem that was soon arrested by a pin-back operation, although Garvey's bookish aloofness was also seen as something of an affront to the Bury-boy machismo that has its roots firmly in the Crombie wearing post-mod Suedehead area. While Garvey would later make a lyrical nod to this – as did Morrissey, rather more obviously – he did-n't feel comfortable among schoolboy braggadocio.

Being open to literature, politically aware, and warmly devoted to his family, Garvey also developed rural passions, not surprisingly as the dark Pennine moors rose from the rear of his house. This love of the countryside he would later share with the band that always hovered closest to Elbow, the Wilmslow-based Doves.*

Guy Garvey: "After my folks divorced when I was 11, my mum bought my brother and me uncharacteristically expensive Christmas presents... We got ghetto blasters, and it was a bit of a revolution. I didn't have any cassettes so I poked around the house and found *Hunky Dory*, which my sister Sam had bought. I learned all the words, and sang along, and until I got more cassettes this was the only one that was in there. They're great songs, and I don't think Bowie got there ever again."

---

* Jimi Goodwin, of Doves, often trekked into the Lake District, a mere two-hour shunt up the M6 and, on occasion, with Garvey willingly in tow.

Garvey would also claim that, by being the first boy in the house, all his sisters desired to imprint their particular eclectic tastes on the precocious young boy. The music that reverberated from the home's one hi-fi system would be nothing if not disparate. Gina was a soul and Motown fan and *Motown Chartbusters* Volumes Three and Four would often fuel a party atmosphere. Sam, by rebellious contrast, was a punk, Becky was deep into progressive rock, Karen was a Supertramp and Elton John fan, and Louise enjoyed a peculiar strain of folk music. All five sisters shared a love for Joni Mitchell and the house's one hi-fi system would shimmer to the beautiful lyrical complexities of *Ladies Of The Canyon*, *Blue* and *The Hissing Of Summer Lawns*. So beloved, in fact, was Joni, that the sisters would often practise close harmony arrangements from *Blue* and *The Hissing...*

Guy Garvey: "I love the fact that Mitchell is quite a bitter old broad now, having put her heart and soul into everything she's done to the cost of personal happiness. I broke up with my girlfriend to *Blue*. It is the perfect break-up album..."

Garvey later claimed the witty, intricate anecdotal lyrics of *Blue* to have been his greatest lyrical influence, in particular the Mitchell method of finding power in every single word. Mitchell could write about a scene completely within her experience, transforming it into something that, down the years, would see generations of listeners grasping and attaching the almost novelistic imagery to their own lives. It struck Garvey that such little novellas didn't have to be born from a landscape as exotic as Laurel Canyon or Malibu; there was no reason why Manchester or even Bury couldn't be recreated to evocative effect within a lyric line. And so they would be.

Chapter Two

Existential Boy

A profound love of songs of a gloomy nature, which would remain embedded in the music of Elbow, was certainly forged within the Garvey household and beneath the leaden Lancashire skies.

"I guess I first started latching onto melancholic songs in my early teens," Guy told the *Guardian* in March 2009. "That time when things get difficult and you start to feel a bit unsettled and don't know your place in the world. Melancholy or 'heartbreak songs', generally songs about love and loss, are comforters. You don't want Julie Andrews when you are upset, you don't want to be made to feel better with a jolly tune. You want to know that someone else has felt that way and you want to know that it's OK to feel that way. Whether you are 12 or 20, your capacity for heartbreak is the same. It's important to acknowledge it and it's just as important to indulge it, because part of the healing process is to feel sad. So these are songs that make you feel comfortable in your sadness. Melancholy has a real purity to it, which is comfortable."

The first sad song that Garvey recalls hearing is Joni Mitchell's 'A Case Of You' (from *Blue*). Time and again he sat in the corner by the hi-fi allowing one couplet to soak in: Just before our love got lost, you said I am as constant as the northern star,

And I said, constantly in the darkness, where's that at? If you want me, I'll be in the bar.

This cocktail of mundane and melancholy, spiced by the under-tone of hope – it's clear that, deep down, the singer's true hope is that the love will be rekindled – would reflect throughout Garvey's lyrical repertoire. The sense of 'being in the bar', waiting for the same person, or perhaps the next love affair, to wander in, is typical Garvey, never mind Joni Mitchell. It might also be noted that most teenage boys at that point in time would have been listening to their elder brothers' Smiths albums, if not James, New Order and U2. An early love for the delicate verbal twists of Joni Mitchell might be regarded as unusually sensitive. Less unlikely would be Garvey's ongoing love for the spiritual melancholy of the great Leonard Cohen.

"'Famous Blue Raincoat' is the only song that he [Cohen] will never talk about. He has never disclosed what the lyrics are about. It's also the only song he has ever signed. It finished 'sincerely, Leonard Cohen'. There is a line in that that says, 'Thanks for the trouble you took from her eyes, I thought it was there for good but I never tried.' There are so many conflicting emotions in those lines. He's thanking a guy for giving the woman he has lost something that he never could. He is admitting his own failings as a lover, while also mourning the loss of somebody special to him. In that song, the heartbreak is losing a friend, the woman he loves. On top of that, the feeling of self-loathing that he could never make her as happy as the new guy. The most effective songs are the ones that show themselves to be honest through their complexity."[*]

Having found comfort in music at a very early age, Garvey's teenage years were coloured by the normal string of heart-tugging relationships. If unable to compete physically or intellectually, he was

[*] Garvey got to meet Cohen at Glastonbury in 2008, within the aromatic allure of muddy grass.

fully aware of the utter complexity of relationships in general. "I used to have this element of retreat. I mean, I didn't see that many girls but, naturally, the relationships always ended badly when it became clear that the girls wanted something completely different to me. So I would do the lad thing and retreat to the gang. To the lads."

Since the age of nine or 10, Garvey would sit at the back of class scribbling limericks about his classmates, be they the bullish boys of the sports field or the intrigue of girls. His first true motivation, however, really did come through a teenage heartbreak and, at the age of 12, he fell in love with a girl called Nichola Towers. He felt besotted and, falling into somewhat pathetic lovelorn adolescent mode, would skulk around at home, writing love poems to her.

"She was a bitch though," he admitted. "She would wind me up and flirt with me until I asked her out and then she would go, 'NO! Ha Ha!' So I'd ignore her for a couple of months … then she would start flirting with me again. That was the cycle all the way through school. She used to break my heart on a regular basis. I think I was 15 when I fell in love with the idea of being heartbroken."

Female superiority has intrigued Garvey throughout his writing and, though ambiguous, would slip through the romantic edges of his lyrics. Nichola Towers might have been the true focus of his attention but, at school, he couldn't help noticing the female psyche being considerably more complex than that of himself and his mates who, by and large, knew little of sex beyond somewhat juvenile banter. Women were truly an undiscovered continent. However, their rejection would also provide him with a sense of existential detachment that was not only inspiring, it was curiously enjoyable. While many would scoff at an adolescent lost in his world of rejection, it was never a period that Garvey took lightly and he would regard it as one of his most profound experiences.

"You know what? If she [Nichola] came over and knocked on the door now I'm not sure I wouldn't go apeshit," Garvey confessed with a laugh. "I can't honestly say I wouldn't go for whatever bone she'd throw me. There's that part of you that has never closed the door; the 15-year-old with the broken heart never goes away, does he? I've got nephews and nieces of various teen years and people say to them, 'Oh, you've got a girlfriend,' or whatever, like it's funny or something. But I remember it fucking hurting at 13."

Following in the religious faith of their mother – his dad remained agnostic until Garvey was well into his teens – the Garveys' emerged as Catholics although, on turning 14, they were firmly encouraged to follow their own instincts.

Guy Garvey: "I continued going for a while then I realised that a lot of Catholic doctrine I didn't actually agree with, so I considered myself a Christian, but not a Catholic, until my early twenties, and then I realised that the existence of God wasn't really important to me. I look at it from an appreciation of community, heritage and culture, I suppose."

Although his liberal childhood would prove happy and stimulating, Garvey has often described his teenage years as "tortured". He certainly garnered a reputation as angst-ridden, bombastic and prone to sudden moods. He was a paradox of emotion; a young boy happy to be blessed with many friends while harbouring a desire to spend time alone. He admitted to being "happiest on my own" and "suffering terrible depression", which he curiously put down to "living in a house with no heating, mould on the walls and parties every night."

This suggests that the free atmosphere of the Garvey household was not always easy to live with. In reality, Guy often longed for the comparatively mundane life of many of his school friends who came from rather more balanced (and, probably, boring) homes. In a neat twist Guy's struggle was centred against a non-conformist background – an ironic reversal of the usual scenario of conservative parents struggling to cope with their rebellious offspring. He carried this through school and into sixth-form college where his apathetic outlook caused him to be suspended on four occasions.

While he deliberately turned a deaf ear to the bewildering ramifications of mathematics, his best subject, English, allowed him space and time to write essays – often long, meandering affairs with little point beyond rampant descriptions of everything. Too bright to kowtow to conventional academia, Garvey once past 13, started to show little interest in anything beyond himself.

Without noticing it – until much later, when he admitted that he was "… the kind of kid he would hate if he met now…", Guy was often a dervish-like tumble of naïve emotion, always waving his arms about and always keen to share some appalling and often invented personal tragedy.

"He has always been really sensitive and emotional," Guy's sister Becky told Q in 2009. "He wore his heart on his sleeve. Guy gets his charm and his storytelling from my dad and a lot of his principles and sensitivities from my mum. I know that within the family people were really concerned for him when he started to play in a band and they wanted him to pursue a normal career. I never once doubted him. My biggest fear was that he would give up because he couldn't live on the lack of money."

From his teenage years, Garvey was a people watcher and was locally infamous for his journals; his "scribbling", as his sisters called it, would be constantly on the go. Often he would travel into Bury town centre, soaking in the sights, observing the characters he saw. One of Garvey's friends, who worked at the Post Office, would become his accomplice, even to the point of taking Guy into town, stealing a packet of cigarettes for him, sitting him down, fag and journal in hand, before returning, several hours later, to pick him up. Garvey liked nothing better than to become lost in time; watching, scribbling, learning.

He would often claim that most of his finest writing occurred during this time; he was old enough to understand the complexity of relationships, young enough to catch the thrill of possibilities. Many Elbow lyrics began with a dip back into these journals. At 16 Garvey wrote a poem he later described as "complete crap". The words etched into the page read: "Walking around the city/Like a finger puppet hippie/Like I designed the city". The line would be reactivated most obviously in 'Station Approach', the first song on Elbow's third album, *Leaders Of The Free World*.

Intriguingly, Garvey has often stated his teenage writings had no shape or direction; they were not vignettes, attempted poetry or lyrics. In fact, it's difficult to ascertain quite where he saw them going – if anywhere. People-watching is rather more freely associated with the aspiring novelist than songwriter and Garvey has often mentioned that this desire was – and probably still is – buried within him.

When he grew tired of writing, he would sip tea and eat fruit cake or scones at the café in Bury market, no doubt continuing his observations or reading The *Guardian*, which he had taken to from an early age. He was learning more, day by day, from this existential activity than when engaged in what he regarded as a crass college curriculum. One thing was becoming certain. Guy Garvey may have been nurturing his own intellectual abilities, but he held absolutely no desire to become any kind of academic.

"I knew from an early age that I would be an outsider," he later said, attaching no romantic notions to that statement. Nevertheless, at an unusually early age he still managed to soak in the kind of existentialist literature always associated with early dope-enthused studenthood, reading Albert Camus' *The Outsider* and, given to him by a friend, *The Fall* (largely because it was the book that had given the band its name). He also studied William Burroughs, Franz Kafka and, most tellingly, Jack Kerouac's evergreen *On The Road*, which, it's safe to assume, illuminated the maverick spirit within him. He was particularly attracted to the rhythmic pulse of the words – words that evoked the sheer abandon of the bebop era.

The link between words and music must have been apparent at this point. More interestingly, Garvey became truly absorbed by the sheer joy of writing and the way it could spin and twist away in random directions. Kerouac's stream of consciousness so obviously speeds away without serious forethought. That, reasoned Garvey, was precisely what made writing so exciting.

Chapter Three

Mr. Soft

As a gang and as a band, Elbow began life deep in the bowels of Bury College, as the Eighties drew to a close. The scene in Manchester had moved strongly towards the energy flash of dance culture, with the onset of the 'Madchester' scene. The roots of this stretched back to 1985, when the city was divided into two gently warring factions: the Chicago house scene that flowered to global effect within the modern grey atmosphere of the Hacienda, and older, guitar-oriented bands like R.E.M., who performed to a new CD-owning generation in the comparatively ramshackle International Club in Longsight. Split almost perfectly down the centre of this divide were The Stone Roses, who proved once and for all that rock and rave could co-exist not just within the same band, but within the same song. The Roses had been growing slowly for six years and their effect rippled down the ranks, deeply affecting the young bands who, fired by the glowing hype of Madchester, so desperately desired to follow in their hallowed footsteps.

Elbow started in a pre-Guy Garvey state as RPM, a spirited if musically confused outfit comprising Mark Potter on guitar, Pete Turner on bass and Richard Jupp on drums. Garvey would later laugh

17

at the notion of an Elbow that existed before he and Craig Potter joined. Pete Turner recalled Garvey when they first met.

"I just thought that Guy always looked pretty cool. We actually became mates very quickly at Bury College ... it wasn't difficult at all. He was very affable, really. Charming most of the time, which I guess is why he always seemed to get the very best girlfriends. I remember wondering how he managed that as he didn't seem that glamorous really. He was a scrawny and pale teenager with big glasses. He looked a bit bookish, which I suppose was unusual in Bury at the time. Maybe that was what attracted them. He was a really nice guy though. Everybody knew that."

Meanwhile Garvey's first musical outfit was named, rather clumsily, Synoptic Reverb, although their tenure was rather short lived and, mostly, they existed only within the confines of the shabby rehearsal room and their own heads. Guy and Craig's entry to RPM immediately caused a name-change to Mr Soft, taken from the daftly surreal Cockney Rebel song from 1974 that would later lend itself to more than one television commercial – toilet paper being the most crass if obvious.

Out of college, Garvey spent his days dreaming of rock stardom. His close friend at the time, Andrew Melchior, became Mr Soft's unofficial guru and was gifted the responsibility of providing those much-needed hip credentials by supplying a constant stream of records intended to inspire and motivate the stuttering band. These included a copy of Sly & The Family Stone's 1971 classic *There's A Riot Going On*, which he heard around the same time as Garvey's first exposure to cannabis. This arrived via a local hippy who always seemed to have wraps of various resins such as Red Lebanese, Moroccan and Afghan Black. While none of the band members could ever be labelled as stoners, these new-found substances certainly helped them enjoy long summer months, sat on bedsit floors, arguing about "direction" and publishing possibilities. The former would see Mr Soft take rough grasps at a new funky sound; in their heads they sounded like Sly & The Family Stone. In reality, they were more akin to a rougher-edged A Certain Ratio.

As a name, Mr Soft hinted towards a gentle psychedelia. In effect it represented an unholy tangle of poorly executed and over-ambitious ideas. Having excellent record collections, the band members fully absorbed their influences. Nights spent in darkened rooms listening to Miles Davis' *A Kind Of Blue*, holidays spent with The Beatles omnipresent in the air, the sight and sound of The Smiths, Joy Division and The Cure. These reference points might seem obvious, but others like Captain Beefheart, Frank Zappa, Cream, Taste, Canned Heat, The Grateful Dead, Little Feat, Nils Lofgren, Country Joe and the Fish, Kraftwerk, The Ohio Players, George Clinton and T. Rex were just some of the many artists that the band listened to and got.

A hopeful Garvey naively declared, "We will be signed within six months", although, had that been the case, some hapless record company A&R would have ended up with a band struggling with over-complicated prog leanings without having anything like the necessary musicality to deliver. It took four solid rehearsals for Mr Soft to gain the competence to perform a clunky version of Chuck Berry's 'No Particular Place To Go', an easy rock'n'roll standard for any bar band to play.

Mr Soft's first public performance took place one afternoon in an unsuitable venue "just outside Manchester". It was an inauspicious debut, as first gigs tend to be, and featured a string of unremarkable cover versions of songs by the likes of U2 and REM. Just one embryonic original song made the set list, a song that would be lost in the mists only to be revived in later years in a much improved guise as 'Newborn'.

The gig was notable for its lack of audience approval, a fact not entirely helped by hapless drummer, Richard Jupp who, on the very first number, saw his sticks fly out of his hands and land near Garvey's vocal mike. The incident became enshrined on the band's recording of the event – a tape that Garvey still owns. The ripple of applause that followed the performance was followed by a vigorous backstage band debate in which Garvey still insisted that they would be signed within six months. This unshakable optimism was obviously enough to keep camaraderie afloat although, in the words of Pete Turner, "It didn't stop us from being shit for about five years."

Although band income would barely stretch beyond beer money, Guy and Pete did, at least, manage to make some kind of a living out of music. The pair took to working in a music shop at the back end of Bury town centre. In the main, the stock was a ragged collection of second-hand and poor Gibson and Fender copies lined up alongside a sundry gathering of dull musical instruments – Denmark Street it wasn't. For the most part, Guy and Pete's time was spent advising parents on what to buy their vaguely interested offspring, confident in the knowledge that, three days after purchase, the instrument would lay untouched.

The shop was a dishevelled mess, insalubrious and hardly inspiring. Its only nod towards any kind of glamour was its very downbeat appearance. Close to the worst beer establishments that Bury had to offer, it was also regularly frequented by local drunks and sundry ne'er-do-wells. In most cases, Garvey's gruff appearance – though he was still a skinny teen – helped to fend off any trouble.

Both Garvey and Turner openly loathed the shop's owner, Big Keith, who showed little interest in music and little enthusiasm in anything beyond turning over a quick profit. Big Keith was not a handsome man and his spiv-like appearance did not endear him to the ladies of downbeat Bury. Upstairs from the guitar shop was one of the area's numerous brothels, also owned by Big Keith. Seediness would abound, with hapless, sad women floating through the shop, hoping for employment and, naturally, a conveyor belt of even sadder deadbeat males, looking for some kind of love, even the cold-hearted, fleeting kind. If nothing else, this sharp end of life provided Garvey with a golden seam of human material from which to draw. Not that he was about to turn into Bury's Tom Waits, but if the underside of human existence is a precious muse, then Garvey's time in the music shop was far more valuable than the £15 a day that he and Turner managed to extract from Big Keith who, incidentally, regarded the shop as the place of his 'moral earnings'.

Garvey and Turner were hardly hopeless innocents. Sensing that he didn't exactly run the tightest of businesses and fed up with his exploitation, they set about, in their own words, "robbing Big Keith blind", pulling every possible trick to extract beer money on a day-to-day basis. Afterwards, they would laugh over their pints as they contrived to take things a step further. The pubs that the lads frequented were largely dour, nicotine-stained affairs, full of jug-eared, crinkled characters at the fag end of life, surly landlords and, frequently, invasions from the moronic fringe, thick as planks, intent on a scrap. It was an awful long way from any notions of rock stardom. The future Elbow members' day-to-day lives were in effect being lived out in the worst areas of an offbeat Lancashire town, with only its proximity to Manchester saving it from true provincial aloofness.

Whether this deadbeat existence would flavour the latter-day music of Elbow is open to question. The melancholic air for which they would eventually become renowned could certainly be linked with the degree of hopelessness they experienced, particularly during the early days of Mr Soft. To make matters worse, rehearsals were not going well, with contrasting musical ideas clashing horribly, resulting in a cacophony.

Mr Soft's existence barely made a dent in the Bury scene, such as it was, let alone Manchester's. A slight truncated name-change to Soft did nothing to arrest this situation. The reverse seemed the case as they now had the dullest Manchester band name since Jonathan King named an ultra-talented Stockport-based group 10cc.

Furthermore, even the flickering of early gigs in Manchester seemed to quickly dry up, leaving the band with the difficult choice of whether or not to perform in pay-to-play venues where everything depended on how many paying punters they could attract. Not easy. All they could possibly hope for was moral support from mates, but mates tend to expect to be put on the guest list, especially if expected to give up more glamorous evenings chatting up women in the myriad bistros of Pennine Lancashire to dutifully stand cheering on their pals in some blackened cellar in Darwin, Blackburn, Burnley or Rochdale.

Life in the band remained disappointingly mundane, with the logistics of maintaining their continued existence fraught with difficulties. The gigs on offer, though normally snapped up and performed with feverish gratitude, barely stretched beyond a collective beer tab that had already gained a legendary status and, locally at least, started to outstrip the band and their music. Mr Soft's fractured musicality, a disparate and disorganised setlist, lack of direction and no discernible image were all factors set to cause considerable concern. Band meetings, mainly held within town centre pubs, hardly diffused this situation and even Garvey's prodigious flow of potential lyrics failed to offset the rot setting in. Being 'off the radar' is a lonely place to be, especially as the increasingly glossy music press were most adept at discovering and highlighting the 'next-big-things' on a weekly basis. All of which made dispiriting reading for wannabes in the shadows.

There were other problems. The cost of hiring a van to get to gigs would often prove to be far more than the performance fee allowed.

Richard Jupp, who, as drummer, relied more heavily on transportation than the rest of the band, eluded to this in an interview for Sheffield magazine *Spirit Of The Times*, stating: "For so many years, just being in a band simply wasn't feasible. In fact it was worse than that, it was regarded by almost everyone as practically insane. The problem was always down to the fact that we weren't making any headway, let alone any money."

The practicalities of travelling to gigs were eased by the Potter brothers' father, Gareth, who allowed the band use of his Volvo, large and roomy enough to cram in most of the gear and themselves. The car would prove to be something of a breakthrough, not merely in terms of essential transportation but as a place to listen to and discuss music together while travelling and to meet, talk and soak in the pre and post-gig excitement. On occasion they would use the car to ride around the Pennine hills, pumping music into the air. Particularly associated with the 18 months spent in that car would be U2's 1988 live set, *Rattle And Hum*.

Despite the appropriate nature of the title, the album proved evocative enough to act as a guiding muse for the struggling musicians. Flashing through Prestwich, Radcliffe, Cheetham Hill and Sedgley Park, lapsing into collective head-bangings in car freak-outs in the manner of the 'Bohemian Rhapsody' segment in *Wayne's World* might not be seen a as particularly hip way of passing an evening. Garvey openly cited U2 as a major influence on Elbow and the Irish superstars' mainstream nature would also affect the band's tentative direction. U2's 'Running Standing Still', a rousing, wholesome epic pulled from Elbows' collective favourite, *The Joshua Tree,* also entered Mr. Soft's set list during this period.* Perhaps it was a Bury thing, for Elbow would never bow to the ebbs and flows of trend or style. They remained positively parochial if their record collections were to be compared to, say, those of the embryonic Happy Mondays or Stone Roses. Even then Elbow understood that music is music, regardless of a lack of prevailing hipness.

Through these nondescript times the band maintained a regular 'four times a week' rehearsal schedule while supporting themselves by holding down, in the words of Garvey, "various shite jobs". These included working in a Bury pub full of geriatrics, chancers, barflys and, at weekends, vociferous youngsters of a football-supporting nature. Again, not a bad vantage point for an observant lyricist, taking in the knots of locals in corner tables; married couples sitting in stony silence, their lives all talked-out; and excitable couples on early dates attempting to make an impression. This was particularly good when one would make for the toilets, leaving the other to sit and contemplate.

Garvey had been there, many times, in that awkward state of attempting to connect with someone or, conversely, of unrequited

---

* The track would surface much later in Elbow's career when, in 2009, they contributed a spirited cover of it for the War Child benefit album, *Heroes.* By this time, the band were confident enough to twist the song around to suit their own style. It was a cover that was also celebrated by U2 themselves, who were shrewd enough to see how they could only benefit from the association, thanks to Elbow's recent success.

desire. All human life captured in a Bury pub. It's something that Garvey has referred to a number of times onstage, on one occasion telling an anecdote of when a rather intimidating chap came in to the pub and bought everyone present a pint, one by one, reducing the room to stunned silence as people expected something truly horrendous to erupt. Curiously it didn't. The chap left with a cheery, "What a lovely day", proving that someone could actually do something nice and for all the right reasons for a pub of complete strangers.

Other jobs were not so enjoyable although, one senses, they were equally full of subject matter, as Garvey noted to *Spike* magazine in 2009: "There was one job cleaning toilets in a private golf club for this caretaker who thought I believed everything he said because I nodded quietly when he was talking, because it was generally between 5 and 6 in the morning when I had to look at his stupid fat face. He was called Ian, and had a long-suffering wife called Jean who did all his jobs for him while he strode around the place chatting up the lady golfers and using ridiculous nautical terms for everything and everyone on account of his years in Her Majesty's navy. He once casually mentioned that he and Jean were invited to Princess Di's funeral but couldn't make it on account of a charity golf match. Jean told me that far from being an officer in the navy he was a steward on a Sealink ferry for six months. I hope she left him. Fat bastard."

Gigs were sporadic for Soft – small-time and subdued. Between band members they managed to gain a regular audience who slowly tired of being press-ganged into attending. Life rolled on. Music rolled on as irksome post-Madchester outfits (The House of Love, anyone?) gained major music press coverage. Almost oblivious, Soft gathered together beneath a wide variety of often rather surprising musical checkpoints.* Manchester has never been a major metal city and, with this in mind, it was surprising to later learn of Black Sabbath, AC/DC, Smashing Pumpkins, and Rage Against The

---

* When asked, in later years, to state their major influences, Elbow would produce a surprising list of songs, barely any holding a nod towards Manchester (apart from their close friends Doves, of course).

Machine being among Elbow's most important early influences. As Garvey pointed out, he was captured by the absurdity of a Sabs lyric such as, "...without warning a wizard would walk by". Ozzy Osbourne would throw lunacy into the heart of a song, a simple trick that would add an unusual angle to an ordinary lyric.

Guy Garvey: "I just like Black Sabbath's music regardless of what anything is about. They are the original metal band although, in saying that, many of the metal acts across the world who cite Sabbath as a major influence really do seem to miss the point. There is a great deal of genuine emotion in Black Sabbath. Incredible riffs and terrific tunes, too. Those first three albums or so more or less defined the genre."

Less surprising inspirations were Radiohead and folk singer-songwriter John Martyn.

"Martyn has a very Manchester style of playing," Garvey opined, somewhat opaquely. Martyn often used a rhythmic method of guitar playing that surged into jazz territory. However, play Martyn alongside any given Elbow or Doves track and you can immediately spot the similarities. Curiously, Martyn even managed to gain a small cult following on the rave scene – as, of course, did Doves, if not Elbow – and it's not difficult to see why.

Other influences of note were the Peter Green incarnation of Fleetwood Mac – 'The Green Manalishi' being a particular favourite Garvey saw Peter Green's Splinter band play live in Liverpool when he was 21 and the mentally troubled Green's guitar phrasing would leave an indelible impression – and The Velvet Underground, a prerequisite for any fledgling band who strive to find a certain hipness with minimal chord structures. Soft were not exempt from this with 'Pale Blue Eyes', 'I'm Waiting For The Man' and 'Sweet Jane' all making fleeting appearances in their set.

A later Elbow influence, and arguably the most surprising of all, was Blur. "They did for music what Tarantino did for film," Garvey stated.

Soft remained an odd unit with no natural artistic course. These kids were as desperate as any other hopefuls, at one stage swinging from rock to funk in an attempt to gain attention. One early song, 'September Sometime', appeared on their demos around 1993. The vein was solidly pop funk, shamelessly filching from Parliament and The Ohio Players. White boy funk was a genre that had been attempted at both ends of the spectrum, from the gritty urban A Certain Ratio to the irritating slickness of early Spandau Ballet. The entire unholy point of 'September Sometime' was to gain a record company deal, and it did provide a ripple of interest. However the sudden emergence of Jamiroquai blew this new-found angle completely out of the water.

While attempting this shallow white boy funk-out, Soft also wrote a sprawling eight-minute ballad of no discernable genre. It soon dawned on them that they should write what suited them, regardless of genre or direction or what the record companies wanted to hear. It was a potentially career-ending move but, nevertheless, it was the only way forward. The members were fully aware that in terms of age and contemporary relevance, they were falling further and further adrift.

Chapter Four

Newborn Elbow

The lengthy incubation of the Mr Soft/Soft period gradually strengthened the band's camaraderie to a bunker-like intensity. Whereas most unknowns founder on ego and failed dreams, the lean years served only to cement Elbow's collective friendships and collective dynamic. By clinging to minor excitements – a decent gig, fleeting exposure on local radio, a line in the *Manchester Evening News* – a mutual respect and genuine affection for one another slowly started to grow. Remarkably, the band seemed to take seemingly endless obscurity in their stride, only strengthening their resolve. The fact that not a single member had a vocation to speak of and girlfriends hovered and departed meant that they could channel their passion into the music.

"It's always been more fun to do than not," said Garvey. "It's not like we had eight years of struggle before getting signed. It's like you can hold down any job. If you've got something in your life that you're really enjoying doing and it's important to you, then you can put up with anything. I'd much rather have failed at 'making it' in the music industry than succeeded in something I didn't want to do. The process of writing and recording became so much more important to us than gigging for a long time that it was only when we got a record away that we started really enjoying gigs again, when we weren't cold calling, so to speak, when people were clapping at the beginnings of songs as well as the end. It's a great feeling."

The notion of a writer slaving away, half-starved in some lonely garret, has always been attractive because the concept of an artist's work needs to be something more serious than a vocation. Rather naively, Garvey cultivated romantic notions of life as an underground songwriter and, after seeing photos of Magazine's Howard Devoto, he shaved his hairline severely in order to encourage a look of intellectualism. In later years he would laugh this off as simple juvenile precocity.

Looking back on those years, Garvey said, "There is something nice about having just enough money for a cup of tea and some rollies, sitting at your desk knowing that you are not going to get interrupted because your phone has been cut off. During our former years there were some pretty grim days but some pretty great days too. There are times, after 'making it', when you wake up and feel an immediate pressure. This lifts when you come round and realise just how lucky you have been. Nevertheless, there are many times when I hanker to do nothing, think about nothing, watch bloody *Cash In The Attic*, go to the pub and not have to think about forthcoming tours or album deadlines.

"Back when we were a pre-Elbow band, we dreamed of such days. But then, after rehearsal we would go to the pub and drink and dream. We lived a successful life in our dreams and it was amazing … There is something that Art Garfunkel said once that really got to me. He was talking about busking in London and Paris when he was onstage at Madison Square Garden. And he said, 'It's amazing how poverty seems in retrospect.' How true. You gain much as you move on. But you lose a great deal too."

Despite Garvey's mild manner he was often subject to explosions of emotion, no doubt born of frustration, which were serious enough to cause the rest of the band, at one point, to request his departure if he failed to "put a lid" on his outbursts. The ultimatum, a result of the kind of clandestine in-pub meeting that most bands find themselves attending, had the desired effect and Garvey decided to vent his more intense emotions via his songwriting, channelling anger, envy, resentment, love and sheer frustration into an ambiguous and symbolic lyricism that would become his trademark.

Cleverly realising that such writing hovers on the brink of pomposity, Garvey also started to lighten his outpourings with small shards of blunt humour. It is a gift that remains a rarity – Leonard Cohen being the most obvious example of a writer who can warp profundity in whimsy, as well as Lou Reed, the master of the heavy subject wrapped in an accessible pop song.

During the mid-Nineties, Soft relocated to an area of Manchester latterly known as the Northern Quarter. Once a vibrant shopping centre until the Arndale opened in the Seventies, it became shabbily neglected until its resurgence in the late Eighties, accelerated by the opening of Factory's Dry Bar in 1990. The area's tightly woven streets and warehouses always provided a darkened, slightly edgy air, which didn't disappear with the arrival of vibrant businesses such as Eastern Bloc record shop, a flurry of pumping café and jazz bars on Tibb Street and music venues such as Moho Live, the Night & Day Café on Oldham Street and The Roadhouse – a blackened cellar reminiscent of classic punk-era venues – on Newton Street, evolving as regular venues for visiting hopefuls and which would become hugely important to the development of Elbow.

As Guy Garvey and Craig Potter's involvement in the clubs around the Northern Quarter increased,[*] a change of band name was beginning to look like the last belated throw of the dice. The idea to drop Soft was constantly bubbling up in post rehearsal conversation in the local pub. So it was decided. Elbow. Why?

In Dennis Potter's acclaimed drama *The Singing Detective*, notable for the appearance of a stunning Joanne Whalley, the word elbow was

---

[*] The author recalls meeting Garvey within the office to the rear of Night And Day, a suitably shambolic poster-lined room that also contained Manchester booker Sandy Gort heartily shouting into his phone.

described by central character Philip Marlow as "the most sensual word in the English language", That might be so, but as a band name? Elbow? It was dull in 1997 and it's dull now. Elbow was a word bearing no intriguing connotations, despite the Potter claim. It didn't go anywhere; offering no scope for expansion nor hinting at a lifestyle, an image or a dream. While one might express similar thoughts on The Smiths, at least that name carried the romance of nonentities. The Smiths has a delicious irony absent in Elbow. Despite these reservations, this prosaic moniker would serve the band well. With hindsight the moment would prove a turning point in the band's history.

Guy Garvey: "It is true that some of those gigs before the name change were absolutely lost. Completely demoralising gigs for the band. Ironically it was just at this point when we felt we were finally moving forward in the musical sense."

The problem was that nobody was paying attention. In the rehearsal room, the band's songwriting was continually improving even if most record company A&R men would have dismissed their multi-genre hopping as a lack of direction. It's one of the perennial problems facing young artists – the industry necessity of an immediately definable and, therefore, sellable, image. What chance, therefore, an unfashionable Bury band lacking in conventional glamour? A band who had surfaced in the more obscure corners of the music press and who now faced a tough struggle against younger, flashier, more malleable units that would slot perfectly into position.

Elbow's debut took place at The Roadhouse. Attending a gig there was always something of an experience. Large numbers weren't needed to pass through the doors to make it feel like a 'real gig', one reason why it was much favoured by The Fall, whose ability to attract crowds was at a low during this time. However it was The Fall's regular stints at the club that added kudos to the idea of Elbow performing there. If it was good enough for Mark E. Smith...

On the night of the gig, the mood in the tiny, stage-side dressing room was suitably upbeat. There was a feeling of a weight being lifted as they settled on the idea that, should this particular gig fail to ignite the audience, then Elbow would finally throw in the towel. The band seemed almost ebullient as they scrambled onto The Roadhouse stage and, to their amazement, found themselves standing in front of the largest crowd they'd performed to for some considerable time. Perhaps it was the intimacy that suited them, for the front row of the crowd stood almost face-to-face with the performers at The Roadhouse, a fact that often fazed visiting American bands in particular. Maybe it was the sense of release at the prospect of facing their final gig or the empowerment felt by performing a new batch of songs. Whatever the reason, Elbow's debut appearance proved a resounding triumph and it was an entirely different band who eventually retreated, covered in sweat, to the dressing room.

With new promise, Elbow recorded a five-track EP titled 'The Noisebox EP' containing 'Powder Blue', 'Red', 'George Lassoes The Moon', 'Theme From Munro Kelly' and 'Can't Stop' and pressed up a limited number (as little as 50 CD-R copies according to one source) for distribution in January 1998. The songs caused a fluttering of excitement in the music press although it seemed difficult to imagine them as integral aspects of a Mercury Prize-nominated-album which, some tumultuous way down the line, they would become.

While not attracting major sales or radio play, 'Powder Blue' and 'Can't Stop' shined like nuggets from the often murky John Peel playlist – the former managing to secure a spot on Peel's respected Festive 50 at the close of the year. The band were undoubtedly thrilled to see any trace of identifiable movement and, even if they couldn't recognise it, the seeds of a following had already been sown.

Manchester's In The City convention was instigated by Tony Wilson's business partner, Yvette Livesey, as a British response to the annual MIDEM event in Cannes and the New Music Seminar staged in New York in July. Always controversial, In The City, held largely in Manchester hotels, brought babbling music industry professionals from around the globe to the city for four days of glib back-slapping or for an intense spell of vital industry networking, depending upon one's point of view. What isn't in dispute is the assistance that In The

31

City provided to a large number of acts, from Oasis to Coldplay, Franz Ferdinand to Kaiser Chiefs, The Ting Tings to Twisted Wheel. Whether these acts would have progressed at equal pace without In The City is, again, debatable, but there is little doubt that Elbow's low-key September 1998 appearance at the seminar was a key factor in linking the band to Island Records.

Island seemed perfect. Since the label's inception in 1959 under the helm of Chris Blackwell, it had maintained a curious balance between eclecticism, with a thirst for underground and world music, and mainstream success with the likes of Cat Stevens and U2. This was the label that brought reggae to prominence (most notably Bob Marley) as well as bringing rock out of the underground and into the charts (Traffic, Free, Roxy Music). Most significantly as far as Elbow were concerned, Island had encouraged the idiosyncratic muse of John Martyn without managing to attain any kind of short-term gain. Undoubtedly, it was also Island that forged the template for Richard Branson's Virgin Records.

Island can now be seen as one of the original indie labels turned major. Formed with the intention of exposing worthwhile music, the label never lost that basic instinct, despite the egos at the top of its roster. The company was large enough to provide finance and pro-motional muscle, investing £250,000 into the development of Elbow, allowing them time to find the right studio with producer Steve Osborne, who had previously produced and mixed the Happy Mondays, with Paul Oakenfold. Not an easy feat, given the band's musical diversity. There were those within Island – and their murmurs would continue to grow louder – who 'just couldn't see it'.

However by the time Elbow's first album for Island was recorded the label was losing faith, having discovered it was hard to find a marketing angle on an unfashionable Manchester band operating within a polarised music scene at the close of the millennium. As Elbow's major label budget drained away, in post Britpop Britain, Weller-style 'dad rock' tugged in one direction and pop cuteness, spiced by identikit R&B, acts at the other. To bring a band so far and yet fail to instil any traceable marketing plan might seem positively absurd, but where in this ungainly mess could one hope to place a band such as Elbow? How would this melancholic music fit? Too old, too young, too sad and sallow, too complicated and uncompromising, not pretty enough in looks and melodies, and not harsh enough for the blackened world of rock, where would Elbow's all-important 'look' come from?

When Island was bought out by Universal, A&R squabbles ensued. Phil Chadwick kept up a brave face but the empty void of non-returned phone calls, the lack of conviction in greetings, the feeling of energy and optimism slipping away was impossible to ignore. From being buoyed by the gravitas afforded to a 'signed band', and no doubt enjoying their subsequent elevated status with a future on one of Britain's most legendary labels, it was a gig at, of all places, The Roadhouse, where the news came in that Island would be dropping Elbow from its illustrious roster as part of a mass cull and their album would not be released. After so many years in the music industry's backwaters, it felt like being hurtled right back to square one.

December 12, 1998
Night & Day Café, Oldham Street, Manchester
Line-up: Elbow/The Drift/Alfie/Stan Chow

Lost in daft banter, lost in Manchester's Oldham Street, deep within the city's absurdly named Northern Quarter. Once the domain of thieves and vagabonds, where you could purchase – at a price – a murderer or a snake, a puppy or porn ... dense, tight-knit dangerous streets, now romantically bohemian. This is where you go in Manchester, as the century drifts to a close, to catch small-time local wannabe bands or, more often than not, darkly clad American breaking rockers, full of spirit and verve, hoping to crack the English circuit.

The Night & Day Café situated significantly close to Factory's post-Hacienda Dry Bar – a serious precursor to the area's new-found Bohemia- is a venue oozing beer'n'fags hedonism. Smoke hangs levelly, at all times, drifting across the space that always meets the stage. Night & Day, night by night, thrashing guitars, hopeful songwriters and detached audience apathy. On this particular night I had been sitting with Manchester DJ Dave Haslam, talking over the demise of Manchester's dance scene and, more or less, welcoming the emergence of new guitar-laden bands. We had been talking live and on radio, albeit one of those one-month community license stations, pumping out Manchester rock and dance to half a dozen stoned bozos in the modern flat blocks of Hulme.

This is how it feels ... in a lost post-Britpop Manchester, with even the stalwart powers of Factory Records — briefly, the unsuccessful Factory Too — and The Fall stumbling through an unfashionable fog.

And so we adjourned to Night & Day, encouraged by our favourite songwriter, Johnny Dangerously, catching a raft of bands amid the smog. Deep in alcoholic fug we see Alfie, fey nu-folk exponents, long foppish hair, inter-song politeness and spiralling rock outbreaks. We are reminded of a softer Belle and Sebastian and in no way does this spectacle prepare us for the Oasis Manc thrash of Mouth, a retro guitar-laden 'gang' of traditional nature, all thrash and pout, pseudo Manc posturing that sits in the thin area between Ian Brown and Liam Gallagher and the myriad clichés that such a thing brings to mind. There is a third band ... Drift, echoing Joy Division's punkier moments, part Warsaw, part Slaughter And The Dogs. All Manchester references are stacked within these three bands ... and then we meet Elbow.

Impossible not to stare, shuffle uncertainly, wander towards the stage, sit to the left, lose ourselves in the balance of the band performing three feet before our eyes. 'George Lassoes The Moon' rattles out to truly evocative effect. One girl dances. The singer looks lost and frightened, startled eyes staring to the café's entrance, his melancholic howl catching a nerve. There is something different here. Can't pin it down — vaguely Americana, vaguely West Coast, mangled with snatches of Radiohead experimentalism. A sound 70 per cent towards forming ... an evocative emptiness. There is something here. I love and warm to the singer's profound Bury accent and am lost to the drummer's clipped precision. Elbow. They are called 'Albo' and a scuffle breaks out by the bar.

Over in a flash ... the band climbs from the front of the stage, smiling and greeting their friends. This is the first time I see Elbow, I am not sure if they are a band of the future. After all that has been said and done in this city, a city post-dance and now post-retro Weller-rock and soul heading God knows where … and this is one band – and not the only one, for I Am Kloot formed within a few feet of where we are sitting – who are a portent of what is to come.

Night & Day Café
April 1, 2000

Sixteen months later, perched on the same stool, watching the same band. Same old smog. Different event – very different – an evening dripping in weirdness and fittingly so, for Sabbatical, the brainchild of Goldblade and Bone-Box man, Jay Taylor, sees a string of unlikely bands performing noted 'hits' of Black Sabbath. It is almost perversely unsuited to the Northern Quarter area, with its Northern Soul shops, jazz bars and dance cellars. Black Sabbath in the hippest part of Manchester? Could never happen, surely?

But happen it does and, mercifully, this is no evening of bland worship and fawning tributes. Each band on the bill manages to twist Sabbath into a bizarre new shape. Think, for instance, of Circus Girls, who attack their task with a Chemical Bros. style dance beat blitzkrieg, or dub reggae trio Black Curtain and White Cube. We catch our breaths and wonder what on earth is happening.

Nothing is more extraordinary, however, than the sight of Elbow covering 'The Wizard'. It is a sight that will live with this writer for many years and one that was alluded to as the Elbow of 2008 talked about their influences on BBC 6 Music (also situated in Manchester's Northern Quarter). On that occasion they would cite the Sabs' 'Iron Man' as a guiding influence on their music. It's not an easy strand of influence to follow. There is a darkness, of course, to Elbow although it is difficult to locate any traces of cartoon blackness or pseudo Crowley-isms.

The evening ended with Elbow sprawled around the room, deeper into intoxication than medically wise and squinting towards a ten-band stint that concluded with the sight of a man standing amid spurting fireworks while wearing a horse's head. A surreal evening, to be sure, and a context that, one strongly senses, will never again contain Elbow.

Chapter Five

Learning To Fly

The importance of Guy Lovelady's independent label, Ugly Man Records, in the scheme of Manchester music has often been underplayed. While Factory continues to etch itself into mythology, it was Ugly Man, alongside the Dave Haslam/Nathan McGough label, Play Hard, and Paula Greenwood's Playtime that most effectively defined the city's underground.[*] Described as "a mess of an idea", which effectively sums up the inspiring sense of aesthetic freedom and anarchy that flows from the label, Ugly Man retains a freshness of spirit that hovers in the grooves of its artists from Black to I Am Kloot. It's no surprise then that, in the wake of the Island debacle, Elbow would retreat to the comfort of such an anti-corporate.

A maverick in every sense (he also published the Manchester City football fanzine *Rodney Rodney*), Lovelady had first become aware of John Bramwell's talent during the late Eighties when Bramwell was operating under his precocious singer-songwriter guise of Johnny

---

[*] While synonymous with Manchester, Ugly Man actually began life in the Liverpool district of Bootle in 1986. It also served time in Leeds, making it the only label to successfully traverse the M62 motorway.

Dangerously. Bramwell had previously served as leader of Ignition, post-mod funksters from Gee Cross, who had impressed writer Tony Fletcher enough to praise them in his outsider fanzine, *Jamming*. That false dawn aside, there was little action for Dangerously beyond the odd superlative-laden write-up in the *Manchester Evening News*.

Lovelady released I Am Kloot's first limited edition single on Ugly Man in 1999, which Bramwell produced. "We'd started to rehearse the songs for the first I Am Kloot album in Pete's [Jobson] cellar," Bramwell recalled. "Because we had to play kind of quietly as we couldn't upset the neighbours, we kind of developed a sound and a method of playing that would eventually become synonymous with us."

Guy Garvey had become captivated by I Am Kloot, discovering a trio that took the raw material of Bramwell's emotive writing and stretched it in all manner of directions. Just as with Elbow, to the average record company A&R. I Am Kloot would have appeared unfocused, as the songs tapped into a variety of genres, with hints of jazz, blues, world, reggae and multiple fusions.

John Bramwell: "I think I first met Guy at a singer-songwriter night at a venue somewhere behind The Green Room. It was all very unfashionable still at the time, a continuum of that Manchester Busker scene. We hadn't gone away because we didn't really get the limelight. That was part of the steely aspect you will find in Elbow and I Am Kloot and, to some extent, Doves, although they came from the dance side. I played a few nights at that venue and maybe a few others, with Guy. I would sing my stuff and Guy would come on and perform a few of the songs that [his band], I think they were just called Soft at that time, were playing. Some of that would form the early Elbow recordings.

"I think it was important for Guy, and this is something I always found, to try songs out onstage on his own. It helps the song grow into something extra, to find its true place. Sometimes a band can lock a song in place and not let it breathe. That why I still love to do solo gigs. There was a lot of experimenting going on and we would help each other out, talk about each other's songs and how to take them forward.

"We also worked a lot together at The Roadhouse and the Night & Day Cafe, booking bands. Looking back you might see it as a scene but we never ever thought of it as such. We were older, for a start, and had pretty much accepted that we would not be chart toppers or millionaires. I don't think that Guy was thinking on that level at all. It was all about honing the songwriting and enjoyment of performance. For years really that was what Guy was about. I think that shines through in Elbow music to this day."

Having shared a stage together, out of these early gigs came the the idea that Garvey should produce I Am Kloot.

John Bramwell: "Guy came down to watch us rehearse and listen to the songs. We told him that we didn't know how to record the songs and I certainly didn't feel right to take them into the studio, I liked the songs as they were, in that cellar room. There was something special, something about the sound that had spaces. Guy said, 'You mustn't change that. There is something special.' At first we thought about recording right there in the cellar, but obviously that wouldn't work technically.

"So the idea was mooted to go to the Isle Of Mull and record the album in this church up there owned by a woman called Pam Dora. I mean, it is literally a church by a loch and, when you're there, you never see anyone … Well, Guy turned up and brought a load of mics and an eight-track. We recorded the entire album [*Natural History*] using the ambience of the church. We were lucky to have Guy because he knew exactly what we'd discovered in that rehearsal room and he was clever enough to be able to retain that. He knew also that the church suited my voice. It wouldn't work for everyone but it gave that resonance.

"There is no such thing really as an Elbow/Kloot/Doves sound but there are similarities. And what happened to Elbow later on owes something to the discovery in the rehearsal room at Pete's and later in that church. Some of it was pure luck, but I knew that we had the right songs with the right players in the right place with the right producer. That doesn't happen very often. But something special happened and Guy was very much a part of that. Guy and Craig actually are very lively. They work very hard and have developed a unique understanding over the years."

Guy Lovelady: "I met Guy Garvey for the first time on a Friday night at a student dinner party in Peter Jobson's domicile on Rippingham Road in Withington in 1998. I arrived at the end of what looked like a lasagne and wine feast and Peter and Johnny introduced me to their producer, 'Guy Garvey from Elbow'. I was aware of Elbow, the Manchester-signed band, but had no sense of who or what they were. Guy conformed to musician stereotype by being a complete and total selfless publicist for the I Am Kloot project. No mention of his own work or art. Just a full-on effusive gush about what Kloot were about and what they were trying to achieve ... From that point on I met Guy a few times as the Kloot project continued. Each time he was generous, kind and open, very much the way he would appear to most people who encounter him through his media persona ... It was Peter who suggested I bring out a single with Elbow."

What might have been seen as a retrograde step, recording for a small indie label after being on a prestigious major imprint, with Elbow having not released any music to date, was actually the best option available in the circumstances. They were still fairly unknown outside of Manchester and to court another major label would have been a lengthy process that could at least be shortened if Elbow gained a ripple of airplay with an independent release. The music was of high quality. All Ugly Man had to do was take it into the indie arena.

Guy Lovelady: "It was obvious from Island investing £250,000 of cash into the band that they were extraordinarily good. But that's no guarantee of success. I agreed to work with Elbow without ever hearing a note of their music. Why would they not be excellent and worthy of my support? Island had spent all that cash, Guy was a very charismatic and good man, the other four all seemed to be cut from the same cloth and [Elbow manager Phil] Chadwick was an intense, smart and focused individual ... We had every chance of bringing out a very cool record. The rest would be left to the vagaries of fate and hard work. The first track I heard was 'Newborn'; it was a genuinely spiritual experience – it was all those things that music can be, something that physically changes your state. Just by how listening to a tune you are set off in a very different way to you were going before you pressed play. Things are never the same. There are songs like that all your life, and this was one of those."

Mr Soft were now lost in time, a mere echo of the past, a loose mess of ideas. The effect of Elbow's first tentative release, 'The Noisebox EP', had long since receded. With the release of 'The Newborn EP' in August 2000 came four songs of curious and unique distinction from a band demonstrating a thirst to extend and experiment, over and above a songwriting bent that, as Island had initially thought, was aiming at a destination within the mainstream. Lovelady had been gloriously blown away by the sound of 'Newborn', and two of the EP's five songs would survive to take up occupancy on Elbow's first album, *Asleep In The Back*.

'Newborn' was the one track actively pushing Elbow above the radar, and it seamlessly built on the structures established by 'Powder Blue' and 'Red', being played often on John Peel's show. Journalists were quick to sign up to the Elbow cause, a fact that certainly surprised the band, even if their (already established) penchant for twisting and turning a tune had started to gain comparisons with early Radiohead. Elbow were also linked, for a while, with the postulating 'new acoustic movement', which bubbled away in the imagination of *NME* scribes, if nowhere more tangible. This led to Elbow being aligned with less eclectic acts such as Turin Brakes and Kings Of Convenience. In retrospect Elbow seemed perfectly at home on Ugly Man, a label that – unlike, say, Play Hard or Playtime – always encouraged artists who were untroubled by the art of writing accessible music. As such, Ugly Man should have evolved into the perfect breeding ground for artists destined for major labels.

Guy Lovelady: "I was given the story of woe about being dropped, the corporate politics, the previous investment, the subsequent interest from EMI, the sudden rejection by EMI, the despair of having no real options. It was fairly downbeat but Phil [Chadwick] shone through with an upbeat progressive message of support at Island, to allow the band access to the previously recorded LP, and offers of support from some of London's premier independent publicists. He was on a mission and described a project that involved leased tracks from Universal [new owners of Island and the rejected album], working with these über-cool publicists and getting an indie vibe going on.

"It would give Phil a chance to put Elbow back in the major label shop window and find a suitable partner who could take the old LP on and give it support and finance that only majors can. It was all very much a project with a re-signing to a major end game. It had a very similar feel to the first single we released by Black which was a mate from school dropped by a major and potentially attractive to a new major partner but needed a cool release to build a profile to start the majors taking notice…. I would have to say the abiding emotion that controlled the decision to release the Elbow single was a sense of empathy with Garvey. He had given so freely and generously to the Kloot project. He deserved any break that could come from a single. Once you realised the support structure that they had generated through their time at Island it was a very easy decision to make."

It was an unusual situation, to say the least. The Ugly Man releases were effectively supported by Universal, which was keen to 'sell on' the non-recouped Island investment to another major. As such, Ugly Man became an effective link in that chain.

Guy Lovelady: "Ugly Man don't do deals, they release music. This was a very interesting 'deal': we were 'given' the tracks by Universal to do a limited edition release to help Elbow entice some kind of deal that would enable them to buy the finished LP and release it under a major label in the future. So the endgame was to see Elbow supported by the funds needed to make a band successful. That was the deal. The first day the tune was played on Mark & Lard's BBC Radio 1 show was a very emotional and happy moment – just amazing hearing something on radio and knowing what has happened to get it there."

"The 'Any Day Now EP' was released in January 2001 with the express intention of avoiding the charts – with five tracks it was too many to make it a single. However, we didn't do all the registering and bullshit that is needed and so, when the 2,000 CDs sold out within four days, it got a midweek position in the grown-up chart. It was then re-classified a few times before ending up number one in the budget LP chart or something. That was a bit special."

The EP provided a second true taste of Elbow's artistic status achieved at Island. Building perfectly on 'Newborn', it was a recording that should have been on a major label and yet it retained echoes of Manchester's underground, a curiously perfect choice for an Ugly Man release. What a pity that business logistics ensured that this would only be an interim period. No longer, it seemed, were smaller independent labels capable of moving within the big league. In a sense, it was a great shame when thinking back to the decision made by the young Joy Division to forsake the fiscal allure of Martin Rushent's Genetic in favour of the barely operating Factory Records. And yet that move came to have such a profound effect on Manchester and its swirling, youthful culture. How much more beautiful, given their unassuming nature, if Elbow could have pursued their dream via Ugly Man?

"It couldn't have happened," admitted Lovelady. "Ugly Man fulfilled a function for Elbow but they needed major backing. They just couldn't have progressed without it. I am a one man show, really, with no resources at all and certainly couldn't have got beyond first base."

True to an extent, but first base did beckon for the 'Any Day Now EP' with its fresh spin on Pink Floyd – an Elbow passion, at that moment – and the future hedonist anthem 'Don't Mix Your Drinks', holding a neatly ironic and ambiguous twist, advising the little oiks of Bury not to take on more than one partner at a time. The song is imbued with a lively humour and was another to resurface on Elbow's first album.

Elbow's situation, balanced precariously on the stepping stones provided by the refreshingly undemanding Ugly Man, with one foot trailing in Island Records, might be unique in the annals of British recording history. In effect, they were saved by the sheer weight of commitment from the label that had dropped them; a fact that might well have been lost on the band when, fresh from the news that their 'signed' status was no longer an option, they had to perform at The

Roadhouse, smiles intact, not wishing to lose face before their close Mancunian counterparts.

But the Ugly Man connection worked to supreme and unprecedented effect. Most bands, following the embarrassment of being 'dropped', tend to settle under a reconvening cloud for a while, lest they face the legions of somewhat envious taunts, oddly pleased to see the demise of a dream. But Ugly Man not only kept that dream afloat, the significant success of the two EP releases actually served to reposition the band's profile. More than that, they even managed to maintain a forward momentum that, given the receding investment at Island, might not have happened on the major label.

Guy Lovelady: "It was kind of strange. Because I was approaching radio shows personally and because it was on such a small scale, I seemed to get to places that Island wouldn't have reached by some mass mail-out. Weirdly, being on Ugly Man actually helped Elbow secure serious interest from a number of majors."

Which must have seemed strange for Island although, as the label needed to recoup something from any prospective deal – money, that is, not credibility – it was hugely within its interest to allow this renewed momentum to continue. From the ashes of a deal, Elbow were suddenly an exciting proposition. Not only had their music shown an organic tendency to ripple out and find its own audience, a full album of, in part, music that had already been tested in the market place, was ready to fly.

Rather than spend a further 12 months touting their music through endless and fruitless meetings in London, the band willingly succumbed to powerful interest from V2 Records, which had been in active discussions with Chadwick and Elbow since September 2000, in the immediate aftermath of 'The Newborn EP'. With an album at the ready, it was in V2's interest to turn this around as quickly as possible. As such, as the spring of 2001 dawned, the debut album had already started to emerge on the horizon, piloted in by a somewhat perfunctory preceding single, 'Red', which, of course, had already enjoyed success with Ugly Man.

For once, the logistics and mechanisms of the music industry, achingly slow in pre-download days, snapped into place, almost at the astonishment of the band – a band who were back in position with a major label and, this time around, with enough autonomy to satisfy their artistic desires and enough commercial firepower to guarantee their immediate future, if not beyond.

V2 were sympathetic, allowing Elbow complete autonomy in choice of material, recording and direction. The new deal projected Elbow to a new and immediate level, offering more time in better studios, with greater levels of instrumentation. Elbow were already a band of grandiose intentions, with the sound in their heads barely approached by the Ugly Man recordings. While they had created the skeleton of a sound, the songs demanded more attention. More light and shade was desired to add weight and depth. Repeated radio plays on the Mark and Lard, John Peel and Steve Lamacq shows was all very well, but the effect was contained within the indie arena that, in truth, never really suited Elbow.

The dream wasn't difficult to realise: an alternative credibility mixed with the mainstream, sounds clear enough to slot into Radio 2 playlists and yet powerful enough to immediately turn heads, with lyrics full of spit and fire, poetic sheen and a combination of effects and feel that would sound … different!

Chapter Six

Asleep In The Back

The live scene in Manchester remained vibrant but was flooded with the successful tours of outsiders, and the yearly influx of students were utterly spoilt by the ease with which they could flit nightly from genre to genre, era to era on any given night. It was now a city of unparalleled diversity within a small space and new bands found it difficult to fit into the scheme of Manchester in the shallow wake of Britpop. Nevertheless, this author caught Elbow during a low-key workout at Manchester's Academy Three, a venue filled with the city's disaffected musical intelligentsia. It proved an intense experience as the band powered through a set of songs that would form the basis of their first major album, *Asleep In The Back*.

The album was the first recording where Elbow were truly able to glimpse their identifiable 'sound', using an unprecedented number of, at times, bizarre instruments. Among these, used to powerful effect, were bassoon, cello, sax, bass clarinet, French horn and wine glasses. Given their tentative approach to recording, such an approach might indicate little more than a musical messiness, a clumsy cocktail of ideas and notions. For all their complexity, however, Elbow never lost the power of simplicity.

The album was recorded, mixed, and assembled at Liverpool's Parr Street Studios, Limousine Studios (Manchester), Moles (Bath), Les Caves des Poiteviniere in France and, most recognisably, Real World in Bath, and the recording venues matched the broad ambition of the songs. Most intriguing was the uneasy process surrounding Garvey's songwriting, his lyrics often scribbled ad hoc in the studio or, at least, plundered from his earlier words. Previous studio time had been dominated by recording one previously written and orchestrated song. Now everything spread before Garvey's soaring muse. However, and possibly for the last time, he allowed his emotional state, and a relationship at that particular time, to affect his work. This became a genuine problem as Garvey found it difficult to separate the reality of the situation from the fiction contained within the lyrics. He even became unsure which was dictating the flow; was he allowing the writing to dictate his emotional state, his situation within that relationship, or vice versa? As he later stated, it wouldn't have been so bad if the hurt that produced those words was merely the pain of the writer himself. But, for once, it wasn't. An outsider was involved and the entire process of making a record, seemingly a fairly harmless activity, took on an unholy sheen. It was a learning process and something that Garvey was keen never to repeat again. Future Elbow recordings would always be inspired by past situations rather than present-day ones.

When it finally emerged in May 2001, *Asleep In The Back* met several unflattering reviews by sounding confident and weirdly askew. The words were welded to a swirl of influences that, just a few years previously, would have seemed quite unheard of from a Manchester perspective. Pink Floyd most obviously sat at the forefront but other echoes were more surprising such as Genesis, Cockney Rebel, Little Feat, Nils Lofgren and The Doobie Brothers. Elbow were about to emerge as a resolutely pre-punk band. No bad thing as there were many musical styles to be found before punk's Year Zero.

With this album, Elbow emerged as oddly misplaced and yet somehow containing elements identifiable with the energy of rave culture. Nowhere is this more evident than on the evocative Floyd-like opener, 'Any Day Now', which could have been written and recorded at any time during the past four decades and hailed as utterly contemporary. Sinister, driving, warped, full of zipping energy and with self-belief and hard-bitten lyrics, it was arguably the most confident song to emerge in 2001, immediately stating the identifiable nature of Elbow's music.

'Any Day Now' is a song of anticipation. At its simplest it is merely the ponderings on the possibility of romance or the future glory of Elbow, a valedictory lyric about awakening from defeated emasculation. "Don't play Coltrane", warns Garvey, "you will sleep at the wheel." It also laid the template for something that would emerge on future Elbow albums – a simmering femininity, an ironic beauty. Within an instant it was clear that this band were quite the antithesis of fellow Mancs Oasis.

'Red' is a sweet song of a person deeply in love, promising to allow the object of his affections the freedom to be themselves, even if that might mean living separate lives. It's the most difficult twist in any relationship, that moment when romance dies in the name of friendship, although it never truly dies. 'Red' sees Garvey's voice stretched like elastic, a slow drawl draping across a sharp and snappy backbeat, a decidedly odd combination.

Written from the heart of Bury, 'Little Beast' is a surreal urban daydream acknowledging the sheer power of a local blonde beauty. It's slightly uneasy and self-critical, with the singer casting an appreciative eye – something he cannot deny has lewd connotations. "The girl's a priest", he says, admitting the fact that, in thinking such thoughts, he is anything but. In noting his shortcomings, an inferiority complex, and writing a song about it, Garvey brings tenderness into the equation. At its most delicate, the song is simply a celebration of beauty in the midst of so much unloveliness, be that the industrial landscape or the thoughts of the men who frequent it.

'Powder Blue' moves to a situation where a drug addict has crossed the line and now the full-on struggle for survival begins. It is a dangerous perspective that, in almost every area of literature, from William Burroughs' *Junky* to Mark E. Smith's 'No Xmas For John Key', the narrator turns into a cold, unfeeling being. Garvey learned much from The Fall, most notably the ability to use lyrics as everyday reportage, without making the fatal mistake of either condemning or singing from the angle of the subject.

As the lyric progresses the narrator begins to find empathy in the heat of junkie co-dependency – not quite what one expects from a so called 'drug' song. 'Powder Blue' can still be seen as a love song, even if bathed in the grit of downbeat urban life.

"I'm proud to be the one you hold when the shakes begin" sings Garvey, as a cymbal adds a nervy frisson that continues uneasily throughout the song.

Guy Garvey: "That line comes from something that I witnessed years ago. I saw this couple ailing in a bar, both obviously having trouble withdrawing from something at the time. She was tapping a coin on the bar trying to get a drink. It was really loud – it was a marble-topped bar. And everyone in the bar was staring. She was just concerned about getting served cos she was so strung out. Then the guy came up from behind her and steadied her hand and there was a little bit of an exchange. He was being tender, he wasn't reprimanding her or anything, and they both ended up in tears; both in a bad way – especially her. So I took that couple and they got married in my head. 'I am proud to be the one you hold when the shakes begin.' It is because in the depths of our degradation, unhappiness, and despair we have each other and that is as strong as any love story ever told.

"I met this girl once who was a fan of our music and she told me her story about 'Powder Blue'. This girl lived with one of her friends and developed epilepsy. Her roommate shortly after became a DJ, she was very supportive of her and 'Powder Blue' became their song, especially the line we are discussing. She used to play it for her on her radio show. She would never say her roommate's name and would just say, 'This is for you' and made it seem like she was playing it for everybody, and people never really knew what the song being played was all about. And tragically the girl who was the disc jockey died shortly after in a car crash, and the song ends with a bottle smash. It's all a little too eerie. And this woman began to tell me why she loved this song and that's far more emotional than the lyrics in the version that I had written. And that happens with songs. Once you put them out there, they aren't yours any more."

By complete contrast, 'Bitten By The Tailfly' features pounding, thrusting rhythm guitars as jagged as twisted metal, with half-whispered vocals and violence. At one point, the song explodes into near death metal and, for once, the lyrics are kicked to the back of the mix. Only after this unlikely thrust of metallic angst is the song allowed to settle into more drifting weirdness, but this is all too soon smashed away by more snarling guitars and vitriol. The song records a bad Saturday night ("down the cattle market cabaret") of pickups and put-downs. Garvey the rampant dog (without collar) scurrying after the girl in the vicinity. Too much bad beer and heady emotions speak of a drinking binge foray ending in a blackout. It's a clean break from the love songs that permeate the album and aptly finishes with a burst of laddish banter. Arguably the most un-Elbow song in their repertoire (to date), it was a warning that even the soft-hearted romantic was every bit as ferocious as the wild hedonist.

"That's a series of images," Garvey elaborates, "but using a lot of metaphor. That kind of writing sometimes sounds like: 'Look how clever I am!' The whole point of 'Bitten By The Tailfly' is to get across how sinister the character is. It's the metaphors that the character is using that make you think, 'How can you think like that, you twisted fucker?' Sometimes it's simple, sometimes it's a lot more creative. It depends on what I'm trying to illustrate."

The title track, 'Asleep In The Back', seems a world away from the wild excesses of 'Bitten By The Tailfly'. Garvey is in ponderous mood but Elbow gel as a group against a beautifully paced backdrop, with plodding piano throwing shards into the mix. All of the band members were utterly indispensable as a melancholic and deeply personal tale unfolds against thrusts of brass.

Guy Garvey: "There's a lyric that often pops into my head, which is, 'Words of love that almost sound like threats'. It comes from something I never finished years ago and it popped into my head often enough for me to wonder what the fuck I was talking about. It's

51

almost like threatening someone to love you, daring them to love you, y'know? The chorus is meant to sound a bit sinister – 'Oh you had to ask didn't you?' I think everyone tests their lover sometimes. I mean, look how horrible I am. It's normally about the time you fall for somebody and you think, 'Oh, she'd leave me if she knew all these things. So let's put it to the test, shall we?' Then you spend an evening being an absolute twat."

One of the key songs of Elbow's early period and a perennial live favourite, 'Newborn' was the first lyric to strongly hint at Garvey's true emotive potential. "I'll be the corpse in your bathtub" it shockingly starts before settling into one of the most tender love songs written over the past decade, comparing the mystical sensuality of love to the feeling one gets when holding a 'newborn'. The song settles into a dreamy, drifting, surreal interlude with delicate mellow organ floating on multi-layered acoustic guitars, with a folk edge that wouldn't seem inappropriate on a Cara Dillon album. It's a song blessed with the intoxicating beauty of a rolling, rural landscape such as Snowdonia or Cumbria, and strangely there is a bleakness that those two extraordinary places can be identified with.

In 'Don't Mix Your Drinks', Garvey pleads with a girl, "Coming cap in hand, begging you to listen". Mixing drinks is a metaphor warning a girl not to skim across the emotions of too many men, picking up problems along the way, weaving a tangled web and leaving the hapless male songwriter somewhat stranded in the resulting turbulence.

In 'Presuming Ed (Rest Easy)', the weirdness descends to a downbeat Tom Waits-style vocal, an elongated mournful sigh, emphasised by eerie backing vocals, dark, demonic and at a relationship's horrific conclusion. This was Elbow at their dourest form of beauty, an Elbow that non-believers would most object to. No passion disturbs 'Presuming Ed'.

It seemed a long way from the psychedelic optimism of 'Any Day Now' to the downbeat plod of 'Coming Second'. That said, two verses in, the pace picks up a gear, with Garvey begrudgingly making the most of life. There is resignation backed by a solid

ELBOW get happy! Group shot taken in 2001 in a Manchester car park, for the *Asleep In The Back* album.
(Left to right) Mark Potter, Guy Garvey, Craig Potter, Pete Turner & Richard Jupp. (Benedict Johnson/Redferns)

Mark Potter at the *NME* Carling show, London Astoria,
February 2, 2001: "I could have been a lonesome
troubadour". (Richard Skidmore/RetnaUK)

Guy Garvey at the *NME* Carling show, London Astoria,
February 2, 2001. (Richard Skidmore/RetnaUK)

Elbow take a tea break at the cafe just round the corner from Parr Street Studios.
Liverpool, December 2001. (Andy Willsher)

Elbow performing 'Fallen Angel' on *Top Of The Pops*, August 13, 2003. (Mark Allan/WireImage)

Los Angeles, 2002. (Piper Ferguson/Retna Ltd)

Guy Garvey onstage with I Am Kloot's Johnny Bramwell.
(Lynn Irving)

London Astoria, 2003. (Dominik Gigler/Camerapress)

Elbow in 2003, at a photo session in a field in north Manchester around the release of *Cast Of Thousands*.

(James Stafford/Camerapress)

Mark Potter and Guy Garvey. (Rob Greig/Camerapress)

Pete Turner, Richard Jupp and Craig Potter. Blueprint Studios, Salford. (Rob Greig/Camerapress)

Guy Garvey and Richard Hawley pose offstage at an invite only pre-tour XFM Live Session at Blueprint Studios on April 3, 2008. (Shirlaine Forrest/GettyImages)

Jimi Goodwin of Doves and Guy Garvey at the Manchester vs Cancer charity concert on January 28, 2006 at the *Manchester Evening News* Arena. The concert was organised by former Smiths bass player Andy Rourke.
(Andy Stubbs/GettyImages)

Elbow performing live at Porchester Hall in London. February 12, 2008. (Carsten Windhorst/RetnaUK)

determination and some background strangeness adding an extra frisson. The tension is released as optimism arrives when Garvey sees a new life, or a new lover, somewhere beyond the despair.

Guy Garvey: 'Coming Second' is about doing just that in a love triangle. It's about very bitterly disliking your ex-lover's new lover. It's meant to be a bit humorous, like a kid strike, a kid throwing his toys out the pram. By the time I wrote 'Coming Second' we were a bit happier than we had been doing the rest of the album."

'Can't Stop' was "a really simple thing we recorded in a dressing room in Germany", Garvey revealed, "so it's got a really loose vibe. Craig really didn't like the shaker on it, he was like, 'Oh, I played it out of time', and I was like, 'No you didn't, it's a big room'. So the shaker's out of time all the way through, but I don't think it matters. Lyrically it's a couple of things. It's basically about a prostitute who worked in this brothel above the guitar shop in Bury I worked at. I watched the customers going up and down the stairs every day and we shared a kitchen with them, so I'd go up to make the brews and got to know the girls quite well. There's a line in this Faye Dunaway film, don't know which one, where she says, 'Every whore knows failure', which I thought was really interesting. All these girls lived crazy double lives. The chorus is, 'They used to call you stumble, they used to call you baby giraffe', that's from an ex-girlfriend, who isn't a prostitute! She's incredibly tall and clumsy, but in a really cute way."

For 'Scattered Black And Whites' Garvey flits back, briefly, to boyhood and the girl in this dream, seemingly in cohabitation, also glances into the past. The relationship here seems almost a culmination of past experiences on both sides of the sexual divide. For this is a curiously nostalgic song that cherishes a new love while yearning for the simplicity of the past, when the biggest problems were scuffed knees....Old friends lost in the mists of time emerge again here within Garvey's experience. One imagines him lying back on a bed while talk-singing this, smoking a (probably post-coital) cigarette, thinking it all over and allowing his consciousness to dictate his thought flow.

"A song like 'Scattered Black And Whites' is incredibly simple,"

Garvey explained. "It's literally snapshots from your childhood, positive images from a childhood. It's sung really monotone, there's not much melody to the song. All of the music is a loop, just two chords throughout the entire song, and what keeps it organic and flowing are the dynamics of the piano behind it, which is quite random and quite fluid."

There is a key moment, three minutes in, when a chord change meets a plonking piano and forces it to speed up before the entire affair simply dissolves into a scattering of images and sounds as in so many dreams.

In 2002, V2 released a CD single promo featuring 'Asleep In The Back' and various remixes of 'Coming Second' alongside two non-album tracks, 'Stumble' and 'Puck Fair'. Guy Garvey: "Puck Fair is the name of a pub in New York and the song's named after it because we had a particularly splendid evening in there, and it was written shortly after then. It's a natty little tune, I really love it. It was written on Cubase [PC sequencing software] round at Craig's house. When it went away to be mastered I sent a little note to Bunt, who masters all our stuff, saying, 'Some more of that distorted bass you love so much!' I like bass to sound like it's rattling your teeth. But of course if your job's to make stuff sound clean and polished, like Bunt's is ... I can remember saying, 'Can you fuck the bass up a bit so it knackers your speakers?', and he's going, 'Are you trying to get me struck off!?' So it's another teeth rattler."

As debut albums go *Asleep In The Back* is a resolutely adult affair, full of intelligent thoughts tugged by very real emotions. No doubt ex-lovers of the principal songwriter must have listened intently, emerging as confused as the narrator. It works perfectly on different levels – to be enjoyed in some atmospheric room, drinking too much red wine and smoking something perspective-altering, or while driving a truck through Wigan. Although flawed, *Asleep In The Back* remains an ultimate triumph.

However, superlative reviews and a tremendous word-of-mouth impact in the north of England and beyond did not translate into the kind of sales and radio play expected of such a well-received collection of songs. Even extensive touring and a bright-eyed willingness to 'promote' at any given opportunity did not set cash tills ringing.

Garvey, at least, wasn't overly concerned. Elbow had learned that the only true way to gain a proper following was to create music that felt natural to the band and then allow that musical honesty to seep through to listeners. "You start writing for yourself and then you take your audience with you, hopefully. I mean my favourite bands are the ones that I've grown with. Talk Talk's last three albums got progressively more 'up my alley' as I got older. Same with Radiohead. I think each of their albums has bettered the previous one. And I think that's how it should feel."

It had become the only way Elbow could operate and, while V2 was encouraging, there remained quite a sense of disappointment at the album's commercial movement.

Chapter Seven

Cast Of Thousands

Elbow's slow but determined rise led to their first significant acco-
lade when *Asleep In The Back* secured a Mercury Prize nomination in 2001. While the album failed to emulate the success of fellow
Mancunian Badly Drawn Boy's *The Hour Of The Bewilderbeast*, which
had bagged the prize the previous year, it proved that Elbow were
making music that somehow managed to bridge the divide between
the eclectic, the idiosyncratic and, potentially, the mainstream. If
nothing else, the awards ceremony allowed the band an evening of
glamour and alcohol at London's Grosvenor House, and even the
slight disappointment of not actually securing the honour receded to
nothing by the time the small hours rolled around. That night, Elbow
held the look of gatecrashers – scruffy, unsophisticated Mancunian
gatecrashers at that.

With the band seemingly in limbo, in 2004, unfinanced by their
record company, Elbow decided to grasp the spirit of adventure and,
under Phil Chadwick's guidance, embarked on a potentially risky –
and decidedly costly and unlikely – tour of Cuba. Although Manic
Street Preachers must be credited with venturing spectacularly to the
island a few years previously, Elbow's venture was a more openly

musical affair, i.e. not wrapped in pseudo-intellectual communist claptrap. Cuba's importance in the echelons of what has always been lazily termed 'world music' remains understated, despite the widespread acclaim given to *Buena Vista Social Club*. Even that admirable movie and Ry Cooder soundtrack did little other than highlight the apparent old-school nature of Cuban rhythm.

In recent years, out of Havana's many bars, several vibrant genres had started to develop. While Elbow might not seem likely candidates, much of their music was powered by disparate avenues of influence and it was through a mutual admiration of Cuban rhythm – plus a burning desire to experience some sun – that Elbow visited the island. Could there be a single place on earth more effectively the antithesis of Bury than Cuba?

Performing in a series of ramshackle venues in and around Havana, the band mixed most of the songs from *Asleep In The Back* alongside a selection of titles from their forthcoming album. This curious foray did, at least, provide a chance to air the new music without gaining instant critical appraisal. In addition, the band's short trek was filmed by British documentary maker Irshad Ashraf.

Although the film would not gain a commercial release, it was shown at a variety of festivals in Britain and Europe throughout the latter half of 2004. It remains unfortunate that this sensitive coverage, which glimpses at the increasingly unique and amiable Elbow band dynamic, has not become readily available as its mixture of performance and loose documentary raised it a cut above the standard tour doc, normally used as a DVD extra and a vehicle to boost initial sales of an album.* At work, Elbow seemed quite the antithesis of the tension-fuelled, combative norm that so many bands seem to thrive on. By almost alarming contrast, Cuba provided a welcome distraction and Elbow emit a matter-of-fact professionalism that helped them soar effortlessly above situations that might cause a band of lesser camaraderie to disintegrate.

---

* Naturally, pirate copies continue to circulate and can still be discovered in murkier corners of the internet.

Back in Britain, and equally bizarrely, the band's acoustic rendition of Destiny's Child's 'Independent Woman', initially a flippant recording for an exclusive Radio One session, was successfully transformed into a surreal web animation by Joel Veitch from rathergood.com, showing the song being delivered by a team of suitably flat-capped Northern kittens.

An unreleased Elbow track, 'Beats For Two', added an evocative closer to the 2004 film *Inside I'm Dancing*, while cinematic interests continued that year as esteemed Lancashire film-maker Michael Winterbottom (from neighbouring Blackburn), whose *24 Hour Party People,* covering Manchester from punk to Madchester, was a sublime work of hilarious 'faction', chose to film Elbow performing 'Fallen Angel' at Brixton Academy (alongside the likes of Black Rebel Motorcycle Club, The Dandy Warhols and Franz Ferdinand) for his controversial and highly erotic film *9 Songs*.

Winterbottom praised Elbow as "exactly the kind of band I always appear drawn towards. Their natural sense of innovation shines through and probably prevents them from hitting the big time. They are a bit like an alternative film-maker who has made it to a level where he can continue to follow his muse without overt commercial persuasion. I hope they continue to evolve in this manner. They don't belong in a bag with any other band. How can that ever be a bad thing? For *9 Songs*, they were the perfect kind of band. It's a film about a sexual encounter that is punctuated by Brixton Academy. I tried to envisage myself in that situation and gigs by Elbow and Black Rebel Motorcycle Club were just the kind of gigs you might attend, if in that situation."

The film's overt sexual scenes did, in the reviews at least, tend to overshadow the true innovative quality, which is the way that live music energises sexuality. Levelly, the sexual scenes of the couple are allowed to overflow into the band performance shots … the sex energises the very act of attending a rock gig with your partner. Elbow, of course, remained completely innocent participants in all of these cinematic shenanigans. Nevertheless, the overriding theme lay close to their hearts, in the way that music can and does effect the everyday lives of so many people in a way that is far more than mere sound-tracking. It can have a positive, tangible and real impact, the kind of connection that Guy Garvey always hoped for and, by cleverly twisting his real life emotive situations into his songs, he has certainly achieved. However – and this is the rub – the artist never really knows where those ripples may go. That is the true message in Winterbottom's film. Shocking given the explicit nature of the story. Elbow as Barry White or Marvin Gaye? Who would have thought?

Such diversions as cinematic exposure, Cuban forays, unorthodox cover versions and even Mercury nominations encouraged the band to take their eyes off the ball. For the increasing pressure of following the success of *Asleep In The Back* was beginning to weigh them down.

Although there are notable exceptions, the rock'n'roll cliché that is 'the difficult second album' still holds true. It's not difficult to see why. A band such as Elbow can take 14 years to edge towards the recording of their first album and then suddenly, amid tour schedules and promotion, the material for the second must be produced swiftly. There are other problems. The second album is the first time that songs have to be delivered to contractual obligation, and it could be that the stock of ideas amassed during an artist's early years flows over to the second collection of songs (as with Oasis, who faced the problem from their third album onwards and never truly managed to catch up with contractual momentum).

The record company's A&R department, such as it is, will be instructed from on high to 'ease the artist' in a particular direction. More often than not this causes intense pressure and A&R often thrives on creating such tension. There are often machinations to prise the old management away from the band and this is particularly repugnant if the management evolved parallel to the band, as was the case with Phil Chadwick. This is important because of the significance and intelligence of V2's stance with Elbow. The label was fully aware of the problems that Chadwick had encountered at Island and the solidarity the band had shown by staying with him through difficult times. This was probably V2's reasoning – that despite the

comparative commercial failure of *Asleep In The Back* and the worrying fact that songs written since that release had been rather disparate
and certainly beyond one unifying sound and approach, it was best
not to interfere at this stage.

This freed Elbow from the traditional band/label tussle that so
often blights the run-in to recording a follow-up album. The band
decided to remain in their comfort zone by returning to the same
studios with producer Ben Hillier. The expectations were that the
same atmosphere that invigorated *Asleep In The Back* – that sense of 'at
last, our moment is now' – would prevail for the new collection. The
problem, however, was that the band entered the studio without the
necessary number of songs, and tension grew as recording progressed
with Garvey, in particular, finding it difficult to write the last four or
five songs.

Garvey fought the creative strain by drinking vast amounts of red
wine. The combination of this and the problems in the studio triggered a downward spiral of insomnia and psoriasis. The latter, causing
the skin on Garvey's forehead to peel badly, was compounded by a
severe bout of influenza, or at least heavy flu-like symptoms that simply refused to ease. Much of the music on the forthcoming Elbow
album was recorded with at least two members of the band lost in a
deep state of physical illness.

While not perfect, the resultant *Cast Of Thousands,* released in
August 2005, was certainly not the disaster that some people pre-
dicted and many would later claim it to be. Without doubt it out-
wardly broadened the base established by *Asleep In The Back* although
its inspired idiosyncrasies would help make it, arguably, the least loved
of the band's first four albums.

"Musically there are definitely a lot more influences," Garvey told
Barney Hoskyns. "Tempos have changed, and I think we're flying
closer to classic song structures than we ever have done before. We
used to avoid typical song structure, because we assumed that was the
way everybody did it, but you find yourself in an arena where you
have to compete if you adhere to a typical song structure.

"I was brought up around church music, and up to this record I'd deliberately avoided using chords that sounded like hymns, as well as lyrics that had any reference to the fact that I was very religious until I was about 23. I would describe it as having a very good relationship with God. I wasn't an embarrassed, frightened Catholic; I was an out-an-out Christian. I lost my faith, but as a result I have an understanding of any system of belief, and I respect anyone who has any kind of code that they live by. Two or three of the songs that we wrote at the beginning sounded like hymns, maybe because of this stoical, controlled way in which we were writing. There are quite a few religious references throughout the record. The roots of most of the songs were put down there. And all of them ended up being on the record.

"And then it was into Liverpool, Parr Street. The sessions started well, but very quickly the strength of the material was bothering us – it wasn't strong enough. It sounded like the last record, and we wanted it to be more of a progression. So we almost started everything again. Towards Christmas [2004], it was fucking evil, the atmosphere. And it was testament to Ben Hillier keeping his head. I guess he's used to the pressures of albums cos he's doing it all the time. Just because everybody came in with a very different idea of what Album 2 was going to be. And it ended up with something that none of us expected. It's so bizarre, you can work on something for four days solidly, and then a moment of clarity lets you all know that it's absolute shit. Other days you can knock something off in an hour and know that it's bang on."

'Grace Under Pressure', was written at the church on the Scottish island of Mull, though mercifully bereft of images of "mist rolling in from the sea". However, the cultural atmosphere of Mull, with its small-time fishing industry, dour religious overtones and tight social network – and local scandal – would variously find their way into both the lyric and the very feel of the song. Something about the undertone of the island managed to worm its way into Garvey's febrile mind.

"I like to wander down to the village in the rain, soak in water and attitude, wander into the local pub and catch the glances," said Garvey.

To be honest, the sight of Garvey walking into a Mull pub is not a particularly incongruous vision; after all, he would have melted in unobtrusively among the locals, who would find it hard to recognise a bearded pop star.

The track follows the extraordinarily powerful snap of a drumbeat. Initially the drum sounds had been cut from a jam and edited down to powerful effect. The band, however, decided to have a meeting about the potential inhuman quality of working in such a way. Most un-Elbow.*

The Elbow members were dedicated to a love of discovering recording techniques after finding themselves sharing a mutual admiration for 10cc and the hugely innovative situations that band undertook at their own Strawberry Recording Studios in Stockport.† 'Ribcage' was such an instance – an odd affair featuring an extraordinary recording technique devised by Hillier. A small, receptive contact mic was put down Garvey's throat and produced an alarmingly effective guttural language with no syllables managing to surface at all. This most curious of methods might go down in history as the first part-tongue vocal ever recorded.

Like most Elbow songs, 'Fallen Angel' was full of ambiguous intent and multiple meanings. The listener is invited to mould the message to suit their own experience. It's an evocative, brooding soundscape that explodes with a curious kind of ecstasy. The song's title speaks about the disappointment felt when a relationship finally fails, when he or she really wasn't the person you thought you'd fallen in love with. The irony is in the realisation that the fault is mostly your own – that you had created an angel and fully expected the person to live within that persona, an impossible golden vision. The angel, therefore, is a creation of your own device; the failure is all yours and the

---

* It was difficult for drummer Richard Jupp, who had to learn to play the break in a live format.
† Not least the vast vocal overdubs on 'I'm Not In Love', which saw members of 10cc, plus manager Rick Dixon and two recording engineers, holding vertical screwdrivers around the corners of the studio around which ran the tape.

person should be free. Like all Elbow music it's tinged with sadness, with the recurring theme of learning to move on.

Since releasing their first album, Elbow had fallen into an enviable state of continuous travel. Well, enviable for some as there were sacrifices to be made for such an itinerant existence. One of them, naturally, being the immense strain put on various relationships of the band members. While Elbow genuinely appear to be a band who have not fallen prey to the myriad temptations when touring in a rock band – they're not exactly Motley Crüe – long-distance love affairs are never easy and, for rock bands, particularly perilous.

'Fugitive Motel' was inspired by a brief stay in a motel in Austin, Texas. The motel was particularly downbeat; a concrete monstrosity complete with a swimming pool that lay parallel and in close proximity to the freeway – in other words, the kind of location where David Lynch could happily shoot an entire movie. It was obvious to Garvey that many of the people staying there – from downbeat mafiosi to streetwise hustlers – could well be from the dark side; each person hiding a dark secret, a deep passion and, more often than not, a criminality. It was a hotel full of echoes, full of ghosts, seeping a certain evil and the perfect place to indulge in a spot of people watching.

'Snooks (Progress Report)' was a nod to blind New Orleans blues guitarist Snooks Eaglin,[*] while the self-explanatory bracketed subtitle directly referred to the period of time elapsed since *Asleep In The Back* and of a band having 'grown up' considerably. The writer had spent time away, deep in the heart of the countryside, starting to understand, among other things, the simple things in life like fishing and walking.[†] The song addressed these things in an oblique way, as well as a more serious subject. Pushing through life in the realisation that, whether Elbow were getting famous, infamous or obscure, it had very little to do with the meaning of life. The creation of music was one

---

[*] Snooks Eaglin passed away at the age of 72 in February 2009.
[†] In addition, the period between the two Elbow albums had seen the arrival of a baby, born to Richard Jupp and his wife.

thing and if – a big IF – the band were to make it onto the next level, that was of very little consequence to anyone other than the band themselves. People sometimes take themselves too seriously, especially people in rock bands. By tradition, rock artists tend to get swallowed by their own myth.

Garvey was humble enough to realise that however good Elbow got, there would always be a down-and-out musician in, say, New Orleans, Chicago, or New York like Snooks who was far superior. Garvey made this comparison with regard to Led Zeppelin and, while he was talking about that band's wanton excesses of the early Seventies, the reference is still valid, for the 1998 Page and Plant album, *Walking Into Clarksdale*, owes its title to precisely the same situation. While walking into Clarksdale world superstar guitarist Jimmy Page saw a superior musician sitting penniless in the gutter; the irony being that, of all bands, Led Zeppelin had based their mega-successful blueprint on the downtrodden bluesmen from the Mississippi delta. It was an important and humbling realisation that imbued both Elbow's music and collective persona from here on in. In short, a blast of humility does a band no harm whatsoever.

'Switching Off' was arguably Garvey's most commanding vocal performance so far. There is a beauty in his voice that had not previously been so profoundly apparent, and despite the slight flatness at moments of intensity, or because of that, the singer carries a fragility which threatens to break at any moment. Of course, it pulls together splendidly on the recording although presumably it must be the most difficult song of the Elbow canon to pull off in a live context. This writer has seen it performed around four or five times and has always felt that faint, neck-hair-tingling twinge that suggests that something will go wrong at any given moment.

"Seabirds inspire me... especially the albatross", sings Garvey, who apparently also had a thing for a pelican as well. The song started at Mark Potter's flat. The guitarist came up with this beautiful riff on his acoustic guitar, while Garvey only had the line, "Teaching her how to whistle like a boy". The pair worked out the chord progression and chorus before recording the track traditionally, featuring acoustic guitar, drums with brushes, and bass, piano and layered harmonies.

Taking the song into the studio with Hillier, Potter eventually decided that the acoustic guitar should be replaced by the Lorenzo, a wind organ. This had no volume control on it and in order to get it to fade and rise they had to switch it off – thus coming up with the title.

The source of the song can be traced back to a conversation that Guy and Pete had had at the Night & Day Café revolving around the dark notion that your life flashes before your eyes just before you die. The idea was that you could choose your last words in advance and make a note, which led to the idea of choosing your final thoughts as well.

"It's a double reference to someone chilling out with somebody and dying," Pete Turner recalled to the *NME*. "I remember before we went to Scotland we had a 20 song demo that we listened to with Nick and David [V2 A&R] and it was like 20 noises or other things were like really badly recorded guitar riffs. This was the best of what we had together, and just enough to get the budget for the record. They were initially very polite, but then the phone call came the next day: 'You haven't got any songs'. And we didn't."

In February 2009, when Welshman and ex-Velvet Underground bass player/cellist John Cale made an unlikely appearance on *Desert Island Discs*, he selected 'Switchin' Off' among his choices – singled out by Garvey as the single greatest moment of his life. The band were astonished although in some respects they shouldn't have been, for Cale's heavy shadow hovers greatly over Elbow music. It was Cale who took a dour Welsh grit and added the melancholic depth to The Velvet Underground. The sadness inherent within Cale's work added true depth to the brilliance of Lou Reed's extremely accessible writing and this continued through Cale's solo career. (Garvey has referred to the Cale albums *Vintage Violence, Paris 1919, Slow Dazzle* and *Fear* as being major influences.)

Cale's upbringing in Garnant, Carmarthan was strikingly similar to Elbow's emergence from the Pennines and, following a classical music education, he incorporated the landscape images of Carmarthan into his work. In addition, the aforementioned Cale solo albums use a technique of marrying a melodic prettiness with a dark melancholy heart. It was a trick that Cale sold to Lou Reed, who would duly trademark it. So too Elbow, who would never lose the power to be gained by teasing the listener with overt prettiness while guiding them to a heart of darkness. Interestingly enough, this is a technique also used by Radiohead, to whom Elbow are often compared – though that comparison escapes this writer.

A pretty song with an ambiguous lyric, 'Not A Job' has nothing to do with unemployment and is laced with Garvey melancholia, speaking of a comradeship, albeit one that lies splintered by unfortunate circumstances. Nevertheless, 'Not A Job' is a song of enduring friendship split by distance, containing a great deal of hope, even to the extent of placing friendships ahead of love affairs. There is a gentle nod to the lure of a *Brief Encounter*-style love affair. "What is the fascination, with lovers at the station?" Garvey sings, before concluding, "You have to tear yourself away."

'Buttons And Zips', as a title, can be seen as trite and mundane or sexy, depending on how you read it. It's a song inhabited by apparently real life characters, each bringing their own tale to the heart of the lyric, and Garvey was very much writing in third person mode. What is surprising is the funk backbeat, a driving solid sound that harked back to the lost days of Mr Soft as well as paying a gentle tribute to Manchester's A Certain Ratio, who always seemed to make music as a tribute to some exotic and obscure genre. 'Buttons And Zips' is ingrained in the surreal nature of everyday life, even recalling Garvey's childhood. A touch of naivety in a musically naïve song.

To put it mildly, the owner of the voice on 'I've Got Your Number' is not a nice person or, as Garvey put it, "A nasty little fucker". Originally entitled 'A Lovely Bit Of Veg', 'I've Got Your Number' takes its inspiration from a passage on The Jimi Hendrix Experience's *Electric Ladyland* – a perfect influence for Elbow, with its vivid soundscapes and jazz touches that lift it above the standard blues rock of the late Sixties.

Boasting a Fall-like title, 'Crawling With Idiot' is deceptively simple. The singer is in a crowded room, in a pub, for example, surrounded by collective inebriates, with the one he loves and "itching to leave". Broaden the theme and you might find a writer itching to separate himself from an indie scene populated by uninspired bands and thrashing dullards. That may be an arrogant view but the backing is strangely humble; a fragile plodding bass holding down one of the most gorgeous soaring melodies in the Elbow canon. A song about accepting one's lot, somewhat ironic in retrospect – Elbow being critically lauded yet confined to indie obscurity at the time.

Deliberately the most undemanding song on *Cast Of Thousands*, 'Flying Dream 143' finishes the album on an upbeat note, with Garvey seemingly content to drift in his surreal love dream. The song's inherent simplicity recalls Nick Drake's *Five Leaves Left* and, despite the weighty musical presence of acoustic picking and short blasts of brass, it appears to be a lonely tune, cut adrift from the rest of the record. Its mixture of sadness and anxiety adds just a touch of spice. An intriguing song that tails off, this is Elbow's own 'Some Girls Are Bigger Than Others'.

One song that had been intended for *Cast Of Thousands* but rather rashly omitted at the final moment was 'Snowball', a highly politicised song fired by a harsh criticism of American foreign policy and the 'snowballing' effect of wartime hype and propaganda – a theme that was creeping into Garvey's writing and that would surface at the very heart of the songs forming Elbow's third album. However the mood was not within the band's sights at this point and 'Snowball' just didn't seem to fit the positive vibe of *Cast Of Thousands*, an album that inspired thousands of festival-goers to sing along, "We still believe in love, so fuck you!"

However, when the opportunity to submit a song for the War Child charity compilation, *Help: A Day In The Life*, came along in September 2005, 'Snowball' seemed to slot effortlessly into the prevailing theme of easing the pain suffered by young innocent victims of war. This would be just one of Elbow's contributions to the War Child series. Back in 2002, Garvey had dug deep into his musical upbringing to recall Thunderclap Newman's 1969 hit 'Something In The Air', which also seemed a perfect fit.

A further political favourite, an Elbow cover of John Lennon's stark 'Working Class Hero', appeared on Q magazine's *Lennon: Covered Volume 1* CD, given away with the magazine. This proved an easy choice as the entire band had agreed that Lennon should be given 'Elbow's favourite Beatle' status (marginally pipping George Harrison at the post).

Lennon had naturally featured heavily in Garvey's frantic household, with his working-class sentiment and polemic touching a nerve.

"Lennon's politicism along with the lyrics of Dylan were important in teaching me just how practical and inspiring music could be," Garvey told Q. "The world was changed by protest singers and, though I don't think that will ever suit my style, it's something we owe an enormous debt to in the west."

Chapter Eight

American Dreams and Manchester Scene

The relationship between the music of Elbow and the vast American rock audience has always been rather tentative – and remains so. There is no doubting that, seemingly in every city, the band's prodigious touring has gained them a steady and growing audience. That stated, and despite vast radio play on the college circuit, the band have remained restricted to a cultish appeal, as if their Northern darkness is a peculiar delicacy lost on the average American kid schooled on Foo Fighters, Green Day and Nickelback. While acts such as Coldplay have skimmed the surface and gained massive mainstream radio acceptance, Elbow have remained one level below. This is something that Elbow's various record companies have deliberated over at great length. The notion that their music is somehow too English, too insular and too intelligent for a mainstream American following still carries considerable weight.

Nevertheless, their touring presence in America has been fairly constant. A supporting role to Doves, for instance, built on the fascination with all things Mancunian that exists at college level in the

States (The Smiths, Joy Division, New Order, The Stone Roses and Oasis adding the necessary gravitas) and intelligent choices of touring partners – such as the renowned Mercury Rev, Clem Snide and Lift to Experience – also served to intensify that cultish appeal and helped them gain a hardcore following that may last Elbow throughout their career. The band would be constantly surprised – and somewhat embarrassed – when faced with Stateside intensity. Such was the case following an impressive acoustic session in LA. A hefty fan approached them and whipped his shirt off to reveal a giant *Asleep In The Back* tattoo, an incident that caused the band to fall into a post-session debate about how their music could permeate a person's life to such an extent. Surely this would be more suited to some black metal outfit?

There would never be any aloofness during these Stateside forays. Elbow cannot, it seems, fully enjoy an experience without finding themselves in some downbeat bar, drinking into the small hours, getting to know the other artists on the bill. It would become an Elbow tradition although, while alcohol is an important aspect of their muse, this barroom activity is not as hedonistic as it may seem. Garvey drinks, famously, but never to an excess that would border on the chaotic. True Lancashire lads; inebriated often, but understanding the limits and, importantly, learning how to use alcohol to fuel their work.

"I have done some of my best writing while mildly drunk," Garvey told this writer in April 2009. The notion is that true gold exists in the flight between the second and the fourth glass of wine. After that, the wine starts to dominate. Many artists have stated similar, including Leonard Cohen's assertion that, "In the beginning, man drinks wine, then wine drinks wine, then wine drinks man". It's the 'wine drinks wine' area that is the most intriguing to the artist and there's no doubt that this is the area that produces a great deal of Elbow's appeal.

While Garvey can glean tremendous satisfaction from seeing his lyrics, however throwaway they might seem, being scrutinised as chunks of quick-fire literature, he would feel simultaneously abashed.

Similarly, if Elbow's music is used as a serious soundtrack to a fan's life, the band still feel slightly uncomfortable about it. It's simply part of a collective mind-set of humility, ironically the very thing that people sense within that music, the very reason they are grasped with such fervour in the first place.

"It is difficult to look back to the great Manchester bands [such as] Stone Roses, Smiths and Joy Division and realise that people are looking at our music in the same way," Garvey told Chicago's *Interstella* fanzine in 2005. "To be regarded as an important part of someone's life, when that life is full of its own emotive ebbs and flows, is an incredible compliment to any band. When you come face-to-face with that at gigs, and especially in a foreign country, it's almost impossible for us to grasp. That's the power of music of course and, well, I don't suppose Joni Mitchell would have fully understood the full effect she had on my family in Bury in the Seventies. Would she have been embarrassed? I don't know ... but I am. It's still amazing, though."

It's no secret that being in a successful band is often not the most fertile environment for the creative muse. Lost in bland hotel rooms, clinging to long-distance relationships ... further strains as adoration seeps in from those that constantly huddle around in blind adoration or simple encouragement. There is a point where the ego of the burgeoning pop star goes into overdrive, needing the attention more and more. Out there people are saying how great you are, how essential to their daily lives. But to fall into a serious relationship while in such a state is never easy. To make it work an artist has to step outside that state of swollen ego and accept a person wholly as an equal. There is no escaping this as the rock star ego is a construction, a fake if you like. Any close partner, and particularly a perceptive female, will see and hopefully love the real person that lies beyond the ego.

For so many years, Garvey struggled with relationships, partly for that reason and partly for precisely the opposite. There was the time he attended a launch – not a rare event, at Garvey's own admission; he would often be seen at launch parties in Manchester, particularly if free alcohol was on the agenda (that's partly the reason why he was to become one of the more quoted British rock stars of recent times). He felt himself making eye contact with a certain female. She warmed to him, chatting all night, with ease, on no small number of cultural subjects. Garvey was particularly impressed by the fact that she stated she had no idea who he was or whether or not he was in a band. How refreshing, therefore, and how honest this initially appeared. When he later discovered that she had been a fan of Elbow all along, he was truly crestfallen. In a complete reversal of the ego nature we previously mentioned, he now felt the backlash. How could he ever truly trust an emotional relationship again? Would that person be in love with the real 15-stone Garvey or the rock star? It was this emotional conundrum that had so strongly flavoured the lyrical musings in *Cast Of Thousands*.

Manchester 2005. It was a curious if not potent cocktail; a low-key gathering of several musicians flanked by agents, writers, scenesters and, a recent phenomenon, chirpy types from the film industry. Holding court that Sunday evening was a loose-tongued software games magnate cum hands-on film producer, Todd Eckhart. His business partner sat beside him, apparently charmed by the frisson of interest in their 'project'. Ex-Smiths bass player Andy Rourke sat to the left, flanked by his manager, Nova Rehman, and noted Manchester manager John Nuttall. The likeable if omnipresent journalist and Goldblade singer John Robb was machine gunning away to OZ It Records man Chris Hewitt, one-time business partner of New Order's Peter Hook. Then there was Ian Curtis' daughter, Natalie, quietly swapping opinions with Granada man Tom Smethan.

Three other people completed the gathering: the author, Lindsay Reade, his friend and co-author of Torn Apart: The Life Of Ian Curtis, *and ... Guy Garvey.*

This ungainly gathering took place in the cellar-bar area of Centro, located deep in the bohemian chic of Manchester's Northern Quarter. Eckhart had already been the driving force behind the notion of a film about the life of Ian Curtis. Soon it would gain a director (Anton Corbijn), a name (Control) and would take its lofty place in the patchy pantheon of rock biopics.

But on this night, nothing seemed certain. There was an underlying tension, as there always is in such circumstances. Curiously, Tony Wilson, the undoubted pivot of the film from the Manchester perspective, had not been told of the meeting. The initial idea of Smetham's was to produce a soundtrack for the film using Joy Division music played by a string of Manchester notables. The cynic might immediately suggest this as being another in a never-ending line of 'tribute albums' rather than an actual soundtrack, but that's by the by.

The most intriguing person at the gathering was also the quietest. Anyone hovering nearby the tight circle, on being asked whether there were any rock stars present, would almost certainly have overlooked him. For Garvey displayed a commendable ability to melt into a shadow of modesty. He remained polite and notably unstressed throughout a rather fiery evening.

"So what Joy Division song would Elbow consider playing?" I asked him. It was an honest, if basic, query and he smiled wearily before replying, "I don't know whether we would, truly."

"I'm not trying to pin you down … just wondered," I reassured him. "Presumably you're here because you find the idea interesting?"

"Well obviously I was always a fan of Joy Division….er, well, was I? I may have deviated from that at some point but you can't really be in a band from the north west and not owe a great debt to Joy Division. They are one of the reasons why people join bands. The way they did it … it was pretty miraculous really. But stories like that give you hope. You realise how much they achieved when they were the greatest players at first. Well, I would love, someday, for people to say the same about us. Look how well Elbow did and yet they didn't really have the attributes many thought were necessary for rock bands. It's all about spirit really. That's why I'm here … plus I am interested."

"But which song?" I pushed.

"Well what would you think?"

"Oh something from Closer probably," I ventured. "It would be funny to see you do 'Atrocity Exhibition'."

"That would be funny, wouldn't it? Not the worst idea in the world," Garvey agreed. "Why are you asking me these questions?"

"Because you are here … because you do have echoes of Joy Division within your music."

"I take that as a compliment. I think there is something in Joy Division that is kind of carved from the landscape they grew up in. It's a northern thing,

isn't it? You could only say that was the same with us and with The Smiths, Doves, The Fall even. I mean I don't know about this meeting or quite what we are doing here … any of us. But these guys seem to know what they are about so good luck to them.

"One of the things I do equate with, in terms of Manchester, is that notion that Manchester bands own good record collections. It does seem to be the case that Manchester musicians have done their homework … years of homework. They always appear to know a huge amount about music. They always seem to have great tastes and that reflects in the music, whether it is Happy Mondays or Oasis. It is certainly the case with Elbow. All the Elbow lads … they may have differing tastes….but it is always really good music. Between us we have a huge, wide and pretty glorious set of influences. I suppose it is our responsibility to use these influences to good effect. To honour them, really. It's no good having great record collections if you don't learn from them.

"I don't think we will ever be pop stars, as such. I mean, just look at us. We don't cut it, do we? But that frees us, in a sense. We don't have any of that pressure. We don't have to be pretty. We have to be real. That's the challenge for use. To use a cliché, we want to keep it real. That's why I am drawn to artists such as I Am Kloot and Doves. Great artists regardless of whether they have any hits at all. It doesn't matter. These people are making great music and will continue to do so. I am proud to be associated with them. I hope, I really hope, that we can do justice to that association."

The evening was odd and eventually fruitless. The movie, which would mutate into Anton Corbin's *Control,* wasn't accompanied by any kind of satellite Joy Division tribute album and was all the better for it. If the meeting served to signify anything it was a notable shift in the presence and status of Guy Garvey within the tight circle of the Manchester music scene 'glitterati'. Previously, the amiable Guy had retained a likeable omnipresence at certain bars along Oxford Road. He had started to represent a secret Manchester underground, an intriguing level of subculture celebrity that might also include bands such as Puressence, Goldblade, Doves, I Am Kloot and a whole legion of ex-members of The Fall. This was a comfortable level of second level celebrity that allowed the stars to bask in faint glory without finding themselves swamped by requests and overly pestered at bars.

For many years, Garvey had appeared in complete comfort within this small milieu. More often than not, his bearded presence was met with familiarity. However, things were certainly starting to change. More and more, Garvey was becoming an equal part of a circle of Manchester launches and openings, where he would languish levelly with time-honoured celeb liggers such as Peter Hook, Clint Boon of Inspiral Carpets, Oasis man Bonehead and ex-Smiths Andy Rourke and Mike Joyce. This seemed a natural organic process that had little to do with the success of *Cast Of Thousands*, nor did it reflect any concerted attempt by the man himself. What was different was the level of acceptance Elbow achieved as a Manchester band of central significance, rather than a fringe act from the northern edge. Garvey was no longer a wistful outsider, but had become one of the principal names to invite to local celeb gatherings in the city centre. Garvey himself, one strongly senses, would have been truly appalled by this process. Nevertheless he accepted the new-found level of attention with good grace and a slight degree of bewilderment.

Garvey was seemingly omnipresent at the events, openings and gigs that peppered the Manchester calendar, such as the In The City conference, held at the Midland Hotel. With Elbow having successfully negotiated the rigours of being hopefuls at the seminar, Garvey was now firmly in delegate mode. He had just returned from a holiday in the Mediterranean where a diving accident had seen him rather dangerously miscalculate the water's depth. His head crashed against a submerged rock and he was lucky to escape without a cracked skull. With blood oozing from his wound, he flew home wearing a large and unsightly bandage. It might be seen as a measure of the man that his In The City appearance wasn't cancelled in favour of a week on the couch, watching daytime television.

"I couldn't believe it when he turned up for registration," said Sue Langford, ex of Manchester's Boardwalk and Bridgewater Hall venues, latterly a regular on the In the City staff. "It was hilarious because he turned up still wearing his bandage and I took this photo [for registration] of his head just from the eyes upwards, a bit like that ridiculous Hamlet advert in the Eighties when the bloke's trying to get his passport photo done in a booth. I guess no one will have that photo ... unless Guy still has his pass. He was charming and lovely ... as he was every time I have seen him."

Naturally, this local recognition was starting to reflect at national and even international level as well. Garvey's close association with Editors vocalist/musician Tom Smith seemed to place Elbow level not only with that successful if embryonic outfit, but also with contemporaries such as Interpol, Snow Patrol, Keane and Bloc Party. While some of those names attained international success at a far quicker rate – quicker than 17 years, at any rate – this entire wave of bands seemed to share a direct link back to post-punk acts such as Joy Division, Echo And The Bunnymen and even Manchester's great lost act of the Eighties, The Chameleons.

On his regular radio show on Manchester-based BBC Radio 6 Music, Garvey often alluded to this connection, openly praising the late Seventies creative explosion and tracing it through to the modern wave of bands. Not everyone was so enamoured. Many ageing Joy Division fans, in Manchester in particular, openly despised the connection and the way many of these latter-day bands had seized the obvious influence without moving it forward to any significant degree.

Elbow, at least, were innocent of that charge. Emulation rather than imitation would remain their natural goal.

Chapter Nine

Leaders Of The Free World

Elbow making a political statement? Maybe. More can be evoked from the title than from the song. After some deliberation, the band decided to call their latest offering *Leaders Of The Free World* because they felt it important to stand up and be counted. Like many people, Elbow felt wholly opposed to the appalling foreign policy of the Bush administration and the effect it was having on the world at large. Worse still to some was the kowtowing of the British government and subsequent support to what Garvey called "Bush's ridiculous, heinous plans".

It was a stance that, although felt by the vast majority of the British music hierarchy, was hardly backed by lyrical polemic or action. Protest songs, it seemed, were something that belonged on grainy footage of a young Bob Dylan or the spirited wailings of the Woodstock generation. Things had changed. In America, at least until Neil Young dragged his whiskery cohorts Crosby, Stills and Nash out to voice their disapproval, it had been largely – and somewhat ironically – left to The Dixie Chicks to put their careers – and lives, it appeared – at risk by their courageous anti-Bush rantings.

While Elbow were not about to transform into Country Joe and

The Fish and Garvey's lyricism would always be too ambiguous to be capable of making any kind of pointed statement, the band did at least feel it necessary to stick their hands up and make it clear exactly where their thoughts lay,

Guy Garvey: "I wouldn't imagine anybody that enjoys our music would be a pro-Bush sort of activist, who may not agree wholeheartedly with our opinions, but *vive la difference*. I think that's the problem at the minute. I thought we lived in a pluralist society where we could embrace more than one idea and live alongside each other. But it seems that the Bush administration is hell-bent on going round the world, screaming Christianity and democracy and hitting people over the head with it. And it's just like, what about different paths, different faiths, and different ways of life? Society can exist comfortably with more than one religion doing its thing. So if people come to the concerts and like the music, but don't [like] the opinions, it doesn't mean they have to leave. If we find that the songs are becoming automatic, we stop playing them for a while because you feel like you've got a responsibility to your songs.

"I think that's the important thing to realise about Elbow. Whereas we don't take ourselves very seriously, we do take the songs very seriously, out of respect for each other with a duty to do the best performance of them we can. And in terms of singing with passion, it's really easy because the music's so evocative. And to be involved with that is… really affecting. And also I'm singing about things that have happened, by and large. So I only have to remember why I wrote those words to summon the correct amount of gusto."

Leaders Of The Free World was recorded at the band's Blueprint Studios in Salford and The Embassy in Los Angeles, produced by Elbow themselves. Guy Garvey: "We knew exactly what we wanted with *Leaders* and to use a too powerful outside influence would damage that. We just felt that we knew precisely what we wanted."

As usual, the band fell heavily behind schedule with *Leaders*. Partly in an attempt to regain lost time, and rather than making a post-album DVD as they had with *Cast Of Thousands*, Elbow decided to ask The Soup Collective to accompany them in the studio, filming every twist. This had been partially inspired by Wilco's sensational *I Am Trying To Break Your Heart* film, released in 2002, which had so beautifully captured and highlighted the fractious nature of the band's dynamic at that moment. No such luck here, alas, as studio arguments are not exactly Elbow's forte. On the contrary, the band discovered that the filming actually helped propagate the warm atmosphere in the studio, which certainly shows in the 'ease' of the general feel. Equally they stood by the DVD, suggesting that it would stand up as an artefact in its own right.*

Each day the band would arrive at Blueprint around 11am and given the locality, they could nip home for dinner at five, see their partners and return in the evening. This loose work regime also helped to curb the their infamous hedonism, although the pubs of Salford offered ample chance for impromptu meetings.

Thematically, *Leaders Of The Free World* belonged to Manchester and being around friends and there is a warmth to that theme unapparent on *Cast Of Thousands*. The vast majority of people who visit the city from London arrive at the newly improved Piccadilly Station. Once through the revamped and surprisingly bland concourse, they find themselves standing outside the station doors, staring at the deadening curves of the 1966 office block, Gateway House, which flanks the side of the rising station approach. Nobody ever seems particularly surprised to discover that the building, locally known as 'the lazy S', was designed from a doodle on a menu by Richard Seifert.

As a first impression of Manchester, it does the city's beautiful Victorian heart an injustice. Even worse, the curvature of the building produces a tunnel effect, which means that, even on days where the rest of the city basks in windless calm, a virtual gale seems to scream up to the station doors, creating a chaotic scene of blowing skirts and inside-out umbrellas. Welcome to Manchester. Thankfully, as the visitor winds their way down to London Road, this unnatural

---

* This is possibly true, though it's hardly essential fare for anyone outside the growing band of Elbow completists.

breeze dissipates, as does the first impressions of the horrendous architecture.

It's intriguing that this most unloved building should be so skilfully mapped within 'Station Approach', the album's opening song. Cleverly, the architecture is seen as a "frozen emotion" within the lyric. It's very openly the story of a man returning home, after a lengthy tour, possibly, to the all-controlling arms of his lover. After such a time away, the familiarity of the buildings holding a reluctant welcoming air. "Coming home it seems like I designed the buildings I walk by," Garvey sings before noting, rather more obviously, "the streets are full of Goths and Greeks".

Beyond these homecoming signs, he mischievously throws in the song's killer line, which appears to be both throwaway and memorable, greeting his girl with, "You little sod, I love your eyes …", which in one swoop, possibly an acknowledgement of the woman's sexual superiority, still manages to sound like a heartfelt love song to a lifelong partner. After all Garvey has achieved. After all he has done. One glance was all it took. This is simple, effective imagery.

There is a lovely, lost Distractions song, 'Time Goes By So Slow', which sees the singer referring to Manchester as it was ("They put your statue up in Albert Square and all the people walking by just there … but Albert just won't do, I don't need him but you…"). It was a lyric not lost on Garvey, who could understand the use of landmarks to tell a tale of lost love.

While the lyrics of 'Station Approach' grabbed more attention than most, they often disguise the sheer blinding brilliance of the chord structure that rises thrillingly from the acoustic pickings at the start, hurtling towards a resounding crescendo where, over and over, Garvey professes his love for Manchester, a place where "… they know what I like and don't mind."

The beautifully named 'Picky Bugger' follows, which, for what it's worth, I claim to be Elbow's greatest recorded song up to, and including, *The Seldom Seen Kid*. It's a misleadingly slight tune, tripping along as on a spring morning; wine plays a large part in this hymn to the drink…. wine and reflection and, as greatly hinted at later in the

album, the songs were written while Garvey was falling out of a relationship with someone he loved very much while accepting the
awful state of 'letting go'. There is a slight touch of irony to 'Picky
Bugger', where the theme weighs considerably heavier than the lilting tune, a trick perfected through the years, of course, by Lou Reed
– a writer who always saved his darkest moments for his most gentle
melodies.

Elbow were coming of age and 'Picky Bugger' is a coming of age
song. Not that Elbow had shown any signs of calming down and
softening the hedonism. The tour norm would see the beer flowing
from midday and it's difficult to ever see this band enjoying rocket
salad and mineral water prior to going onstage. Part of the Elbow
appeal is based on a lifestyle that, at times, might stretch even
Lemmy's limitations.

'Forget Myself' places the narrator back in Manchester's Piccadilly.
It could be 'Station Approach (Slight Return)' as the thunderous
chords of the opening track return in thinly disguised form.* Again
geographical imagery is used to great effect; the singer builds his own
emotions into buildings that flash by, both in the city centre and the
satellite towns. There is even a touch of Peter Ackroyd here, albeit a
Northern version, where ghosts and echoes of the past linger on
every street corner.

'The Stops' describes the end of the affair, in this case, as has been
widely reported, Garvey's relationship with BBC Radio 1 DJ Edith
Bowman. "I'll miss you the way you miss the sea," he openly sings on
this most heartfelt of songs, implying that the greatest hurt lies on his
side. By the time the song was released and flickered briefly on, ironically, Radio 1, Garvey had already moved on while Bowman had
taken up with Garvey's good friend Tom Smith, of Editors. Like a
great photograph or emotive painting, the moment is captured and
prettily contained, despite the pain that lingers.

"Edith and I were in a relationship for about a year," Garvey

---

* It would have made for a classic seven-inch single, with Part Two on the flip as
in 'Layla' or 'Oh Well'.

confirmed. "And at the time that I wrote 'The Stops' it had become apparent that it wasn't working for one reason or another. And whereas most post-relationship love songs are either mournful and sort of sad, this one is sad that it hasn't worked, but the chorus is sort of stating that I was really glad that it happened, and I'm really glad that we did try. And I'll have Edith in my life in one way or another for the rest of it, because she's great. I like it because it isn't one way or another. That's not the nature of real life. You can have a relationship with somebody in this day and age and it might not work but you can still love each other and still be friends. And there are a number of people I know who have a really, really special relationship because they share a child or something like that. I don't like just black and white romance. It has to be realistic."

The title track, 'Leaders Of The Free World', begins in fun as a rehearsal utilised as a song intro. A dat-dat-dat, bum-bum-bum rhythm carries the listener to the heart of typical Garvey angst. The line used in throwaway fashion describes the 'leaders' as being "little boys throwing stones". The overall theme attains an increasingly angry touch like "the Sixties didn't happen" – the point being that man is condemned to keep repeating the mistakes of the past. Around and around it goes, a thundering rolling tank of a song and undoubtedly the angriest from a band that don't, as a rule, trade in angry songs.

Those who believe a linear path runs from Joy Division to Elbow might point to 'An Imagined Affair' as evidence. A sad, faintly sinister tale of male loneliness and, as the title strongly suggests, a life of love lived wholly in the imagination, the lyric spills into a trickle of surreal images hovering precariously between innocent and lustful. At one point, Garvey even admits, "These feelings belong in a zoo." The whole affair seems little more than the angst felt by a lonely man as a beautiful girl drifts by, arm in arm with someone else. In terms of poetic imagery, it's only slightly beyond Joe Jackson's barroom level rant, 'Is She Really Going Out With Him', yet softer, darker. The man is not necessarily so pathetic and, as per usual, ends up talking crap in some downbeat bar. Most men can acquaint with this.

Guy Garvey at the first of two sold out homecoming shows at Manchester Apollo on October 23, 2008.

(Shirlaine Forrest/GettyImages)

Guy Garvey at the Reading Festival, August 30, 2005. (Andy Willsher)

Elbow at 'Get Loaded in The Park', August 28, 2005. (Craig Dunsmuir/GettyImages)

Craig Potter performs in the aftermath the success of *The Seldom Seen Kid* at the Manchester Academy on April 13, 2008. (Shirlaine Forrest/GettyImages)

Mark Potter, Guy Garvey, Richard Jupp and Pete Turner at the Manchester Academy.

(Shirlaine Forrest/GettyImages)

— elbow —

Set List Blueprint 3rd April 2008

STARLINGS
BONES
LEADERS
GREAT EXPETATIONS
~~▬▬▬▬▬~~

MIRROR BALL
RED
GROUNDS
THE FIX
TOWER CRANE
THE STOPS
NEW BORN
ONE DAY
FORGET MYSELF

STATION APPROACH
GRACE UNDER PRESSURE

is only a genuine setlist if this is written on it

(Top left) Set list of Elbow's performance at invite Live Session at Blueprint Studios on April 3, 2008.
Guy Garvey (top right), Mark Potter (bottom left), Pete Turner (bottom right) at the Blueprint Studios session.
(Shirlaine Forrest/GettyImages)

Stephen Fretwell with Elbow perform at the Night and Day café in north Manchester, January 16, 2008.
(Shirlaine Forrest/GettyImages)

Richard Jupp and Elbow at Night and Day café on January 16, 2008. (Shirlaine Forrest/GettyImages)

Richard Hawley, who played guitar on 'The Fix', from *The Seldom Seen Kid*, Glastonbury, 2008. (Andy Willsher)

Elbow, by now one of Britain's classic festival acts, on stage at Glastonbury, 2008. (Andy Willsher)

Guy Garvey at home in Manchester. May 30, 2008. (Ed Westmacott/RetnaUK)

Brimming with confidence after winning two Ivor Novello Awards, 2009.
(Left to right) Richard Jupp, Mark Potter, Guy Garvey, Pete Turner & Craig Potter. (LFI)

Elbow enjoy their supreme moment at the Mercury Music Prize, 2008. (LFI)

'Mexican Standoff' is a simple emotion – the natural hatred felt towards the man she has left you for. Women, one strongly senses, can also relate strongly to this. Yet, for all that, 'Mexican Standoff' is a song of foolish machismo, which even admits to the fact that "he is better looking than me". The song employs an effective Sixties beat combo feel, complete with twanging Hank Marvin-esque guitar that growls beneath the vocal line, which drifts rather edgily from its already plodding central melody. The whole song crashes to a middle eight before speeding away like the titles of an old cop or spy movie.

Simplicity continues to dominate the thematic nature of *Leaders Of The Free World* and despite the complexity of the arrangement, 'The Everthere' is no exception. The question posed in the song is simple and timeworn: when this glory fades, will you still be there? Garvey's level of fame might diminish so what might lie beyond that level of celebrity. Does the old Guy lurk there or has he gone forever?

Again, 'My Very Best' is said to concern the end of the affair with Edith Bowman. Whether that's the case or not, this is another song that evokes the heightened state of heartbreak. When heartbroken it is often said that the world turns to grey, loses its magic but, in doing precisely that, it still becomes unreal. "You've gone and made a beautiful hole in my heart" is, if nothing else, a refreshing way of accentuating the positive in a seemingly hopeless situation.

'Great Expectations' is a strange one – for this writer anyway. It isn't just the memorable line about the "Stockport supporters club" that reminds me of my old home town. The entire song seems drizzled upon in the Stockport manner. A love story acted out on a damp Tuesday in Edgeley, where born-again Christians flutter behind lace curtains. 'Great Expectations' is a tale of an old friendship that was never without a love that simmers under the surface.

'Puncture Repair' is an admission of guilt, the knowledge that you have hurt someone and possibly deliberately. Not a comfortable emotion to live with although the protagonist in the song seems forever forgiving. Which is just as well.

★

Released in October 2005, *Leaders Of The Free World* appeared to a glut of positive reviews, becoming the album that many still regard as Elbow's finest. Unfortunately this again failed to translate into sales and while allowing the band artistic freedom was seen as an outward vote of confidence from V2, problems soon arose between band and label.

The company had never been altogether comfortable with Phil Chadwick, preferring to put their own idea of a manager in place. Chadwick was welded to the band via a long-term friendship and this created an immediate 'us and them' situation.

One V2 employee who prefers to remain anonymous because he wishes to work with Elbow again, revealed, "It was frustrating. We knew this could be the biggest band in the world. Well that's what we thought but, for all their brilliance, there remained a small-town mentality about Elbow that you would never have found with U2."

A fantastic – and revealing – statement. Elbow's refusal to become another U2 is the very reason they were 'brilliant' in the first place. To evolve into a world-sized act of U2 or Coldplay proportions would simply be to create a completely different band out of the core of Elbow. It has happened many times, of course, and there is a potent industry argument that would claim that this is the 'only' way to progress. Either that or take an immediate road out, either by splitting after the second album or worse, as in Joy Division or Nirvana's case. The notion that you can only seal a state of artistic perfection before moving on and, inevitably, 'softening' isn't an absolute rule, as Cohen, Dylan, Reed, Young etc might suggest. But it is the norm.

Looked at in terms of simple mathematics, *Leaders Of The Free World* did not sell well enough to continue the level of record company investment. Given the disintegrating state of the music business a band had to build steadily and other Elbow contemporaries had managed to achieve this. Editors' steady growth might have seemed stoic to outside eyes, but their work rate and constant chipping away at the world circuit would see their sales graph continuing to rise. Likewise Interpol, The Killers, Muse – all bands rising from a cult base. But not so Elbow. V2 employees could be forgiven for noting the dipping nature of a graph that, despite the excellence of the music, actually started to fall away rapidly after the first month of sales.

Worse still, *Cast Of Thousands*, an inferior album in so many areas, could now be seen as the Elbow benchmark. Not difficult, either to see an ageing band moving steadily away from any notions of pulse beat. V2 simply could not afford to maintain a steady seller … Elbow had to blast through that particular commercial fog. Could they be blamed for backtracking? Not really. Ripples of discontent ran through the company and an urge to find younger, edgier music was not helping matters. Even the DVD, skilfully produced with The Soup Collective, which gained further positive critical notices, failed to arrest the decline.

In the summer of 2006, Elbow once again ventured Stateside and further north to the uncharted commercial territory of Canada. Here they discovered an urban audience with an industrial heritage of their own, and several frenetic college interviews hinted at a certain level of intensity within their growing following. Elbow seemed strangely suited to Canada, or at least urban Canada (they had always enjoyed the most northerly American cities too, Chicago and Boston in particular), where they seemed to discover an unexpected kinship.

Perhaps this cold, damp, vast country shared its evocative imagery with the bleakness of the Pennines? Maybe the very look of the band, complete with Garvey's hirsute appearance – like that of The Band – seemed to match the Canadian image. Whatever the reason, an understanding had been growing with intent for several years – Canucks enjoying and seemingly understanding Garvey's dark surrealism.

It may seem a ludicrous notion – that a band's music reflects the landscape in which it was created – but it does often seem so. It's not difficult to sense this Canadian connection, which might become lost in translation in LA for example. To put it simply, Elbow's is not beach blanket bingo music.

The band headlined the Ukula Bright Lights Festival in Toronto's distillery district, amid a grid-like entanglement of darkened warehouses, watched by a not entirely glamorous mix of students and check-shirted blue-collar Americans. The connection between Garvey's lyrics and the Manchester landscape was remarked upon immediately before the show.

"I think the lyrics are one of the tools of the box in order to get your feelings across," said Garvey. "I don't think it matters if you use local imagery as long as it's part of the bigger picture."

The statement seemed to be fully backed up by the band's onstage rendition of 'Station Approach', as equally at home in the untested Toronto streets as in Manchester's Piccadilly.

If *Leaders Of The Free World* had been an artistic triumph, gaining multitudinous plaudits across the globe and seeping steadily, if unspectacularly, into a global fan base, could Elbow be the world's best kept secret? To their satisfaction, stardom had been avoided by the use of a stealth-like precision, a feat that might not seem so difficult in the modern world. Celebrity was no longer the domain of the very gifted and an idiosyncratic talent such as Elbow's would prove a positive disadvantage in a world postulating with miniskirted wannabes blessed with varying and often invisible degrees of ability.

Did that, therefore, make Elbow cultishly global in the manner of, say, The Pixies who, in their prime, could fill large venues across the globe and yet be virtually unrecognised offstage? Elbow as reluctant heroes? Even that title – this book's title – can seem rather patronising.

The problem with this would be obvious to every record company executive who still believes in the maxim set in stone by Maurice Oberstein, the legendary CBS Head of Marketing, who famously stated, "Art is for artists. Running a record company is all about shifting black vinyl."

Although technology would soon date that statement in a number of ways, the cynical fact remains the same. This wouldn't be such a problem with minority or specialist artists who often find a home on a suitably esoteric label. The rise of the internet has had a hugely beneficial effect, linking these smaller genres directly with label heads and, most importantly, fans. The problem occurs with artists whose own output criss-crosses categories, with a stubborn reluctance to be pigeonholed. Soon, even the largest megastores would loosely file these acts under the 'rock and pop' sections, which, themselves, would be under threat from games and DVDs.

Elbow's marketing position had always been uncomfortable. Radio stations were equally nervous about them, though not so much in the UK, where they became snug regulars on the national play lists of both Radio 1 (and subsequent youth-orientated national stations such as BBC 6 Music) and the liberally middle-aged Radio 2.

Garvey's extra-curricular activities might also seem to run slightly against the rock'n'roll grain. A 'twitcher' from an early age (most enthusiasts begin when in older years), he developed a lifelong passion for bird-watching that he shared with his friend Jimi Goodwin from Doves. Garvey delighted in watching the falcons swooping over Manchester and took more than a degree of inspiration from such sights of extraordinary beauty circulating around the city's unloved industrial buildings. This was no fleeting interest either, as Garvey's constant trips to the Lakes and, on one infamous occasion, to catch sight of the Red Kites at Tregaron, mid Wales, proved.

Having produced I Am Kloot's first album, in 2005, Garvey returned to the studio with them as co-producer of their excellent limited edition single, 'Maybe I Should', written by John Bramwell. Garvey's time with Kloot allowed him to languish in a laddish camaraderie that was not directly connected with the problems of Elbow. As A&R director and co-owner of I Am Kloot label, Skinny Dog, Garvey was able to indulge in the mechanics of the indie scene.

"I envy Kloot to some extent," he said at the time. "Partly because I believe they are one of the greatest British bands of the past 30 years, without doubt, but also because they are free from the levels of expectation that we [Elbow] have had to contend with. It's ironic because I am part of the reason for that. All the more ironic, I guess, because Kloot would surely swap places with Elbow … I don't know, we haven't talked that much about that side of it. It's curious but, at the time, Kloot were truly inspirational in every possible way … and I have always found working with them to be truly inspirational."

John Bramwell: "Skinny Dog is not a label as such. But we can put out somebody's first single and then a lot of the time it is up to them. Pete [Jobson] is far more involved than I am. It is separate from Kloot, really. Kloot are licensed all over the world. It always worked for us because we craved that sense of autonomy. Not sure it could have worked for Elbow. Guy Garvey is involved, if a bit loosely ... but it's something that is what it is, really. I think that Guy loves the idea of helping to get more music through, as do I. It is something that will grow ... well hopefully it will transcend Kloot. But it works perfectly well for us."[*]

After all the critical success and ground gained, it still seemed that Elbow's progress was to be unsteady in the wake of *Leaders Of The Free World*, a frustration only countered by the fact that *Leaders* had actually increased the band's momentum. It was out of the hands of record company or band – while the album never became a mega-seller, it continued to grow and, partly to V2's surprise, also started to reactivate sales of Elbow's back catalogue, something that may have caused the legal wrangles to intensify. For this was no sad squabble over a lame duck act, all but finished as a genuine force.

There was still a feeling that something momentous could happen – although this was hardly apparent as the band booked themselves back into Blueprint Studios to begin tentative work on their next album. The sound that had embellished *Leaders* would be perfect this time around, even if the band had a rather more grandiose approach in mind, whether or not it would ever reach a state of mainstream release.

Craig Potter: "It does seem to have been a long time since the last album and that has been rather frustrating for us all. We have been writing songs ... getting them together pretty much all the time. We have been in the studio at various times, picking up songs where we left them and it's the first chance we've had to do that. The songs may

[*] As of writing, Guy Garvey is producing the fifth I Am Kloot album, due in autumn 2009.

90

have been different had we just gone in and done them in one fell swoop. It's just the way things panned out ... There was a long period when we were in limbo and it is difficult to focus when you don't know where you are. We knew we would get a deal but it's strange when you are not sure who it will be with and you can't be sure of the timescale. That makes it a different process entirely ... I think if it had all been done earlier then the album would've been done earlier. There was no rush to finish the record and I think in the end it paid off."

To some extent, the lack of record company support would prove a bonus. Not so for some debutante artists, dogged by uncertainty and the dark prospect of a prompt return to obscurity, but Elbow could be pretty sure that, once the legal dust settled, a solid deal could be found. In truth Elbow had made just enough money to ride out the legal wrangles that lasted a full two years and, as they continued recording, things became rather fractious as the money finally started to dry up. Having been eventually freed from V2, the band were on the verge of signing a new deal which fell through due to further legalities. Confidence started to dip. The members had families, commitments and far from joyously recording the album they were destined to make, the band were literally teetering on the brink of pulling out of the studio, selling unnecessary equipment and falling into a spell of gigging in order to survive.

The subsequent deal the band signed with Fiction Records could not have arrived at a more opportune moment, just as the band were a couple of weeks way from taking drastic action, although one mind-numbing irony was not lost on Elbow and explains much about the bewildering cogs and wheels of the music industry. Fiction – a label that for decades had always operated an open, honest and perceptive A&R policy – was now part of Universal, the very same company that dropped the band when it bought Island Records in 1988.

"In fact the same guy who sacked us is now head of the company," Garvey noted in the *Guardian*. "When they [Island] dropped us I phoned his voicemail and said, 'Obviously I am disappointed but it's been nice working with you, take care of yourself.' Who knows, maybe he wouldn't have had us back if I had called up and gone, 'You cunts'."

The album was almost finished with only one track remaining to be taped. Ironically, it would become the album's most impressive moment and biggest hit, and signified an upturn in spirit within the band. Unusually for Elbow, they opted for convention. This song would make people happy.

Chapter Ten

The Seldom Seen Kid

As Elbow left manager Phil Chadwick to negotiate the new deal with Fiction, the band finalised what would become the most important English rock album since Oasis' thunderous debut, *Definitely Maybe* – a comparison of commercial and cultural effect, rather than aesthetic parallel. While Oasis caused the scramble back to guitars in the wake of the rave uprising, theirs was a basic rock'n'roll phenomenon. Elbow, by contrast, would gain mainstream success for an entirely more complex art form.

Songs had filled the Garvey notebook. Scribbles and rants, heady emotions and one-off instant thoughts. Songs of life, death, boredom and thoughtful exuberance – same as ever, except this time the emotive power would be matched by a gargantuan notion of sound.

The Seldom Seen Kid was, as stated in an earlier chapter, Bryan Glancy, and the themes that form to make the whole of this, Elbow's monumental statement to date, were drawn from a two-year period that hinged on the death of 39-year-old Glancy on 20 January, 2006. The significance of his sudden demise became apparent in the immediate aftermath as tributes poured onto a memorial website. A friend had faded and in doing so, immediately became larger than life. For

Elbow, it was far more than that. The importance of their muse suddenly seemed lost. Bryan had gone.

Fittingly, *The Seldom Seen Kid* is not a particularly rock'n'roll record, rather a reaffirmation of the self, dealing directly with a sense of loss, and is more profound than could be imagined. The suddenness of the death of a friend leaves a sense of the surreal – dizziness, emptiness, an ethereal floating space. Such is the theme of 'The Seldom Seen Kid'. Garvey writes of walking through deserted Bury streets on a Sunday afternoon, memories flooding through his mind. Everything from privet hedges to a telephone box carrying a memory, never more sensitive than in the wake of loss.

The thematic base of opener 'Starlings', with its flippant and throwaway opening line, "How dare the Premier ignore my invitations? He'll have to go ..." sees Garvey attempting to conjure forth a character rather like Radio 4's curmudgeonly old fart Count Arthur Strong, a fictional persona created by English comedian Steve Delaney. Garvey's creation can be seen as belligerent, faintly pompous and self-important.

Garvey's notion, "that [his alter ego in the song] is something of an exaggeration of a part of my own character that I have to keep in check", certainly seems to ring true for he has surfaced before, if not in entire songs then certainly in fleeting moments.

The song is intriguingly self-examining. The central character is semi successful, lost in his bloated ego and yet is crushed by the sudden appearance of unexpected beauty, in this case a waitress. The almost violent blast of horns that begins the song signifies that particular sexual submission, that flash of a moment when beauty knocks you sideways, rendering you utterly helpless, at least for a few elongated moments.

It's a recurring theme within the spectrum of modern songwriting, with the character of a waitress making appearances in songs by other artists such as Bob Dylan and Tom Waits. Waitresses provided a muse that triggered many of Waits' early songs, although they would be symbolic of an uncaring world whereas, on 'Starlings', Garvey feels a rush of love, rather than lust. The black-clad waitresses of

England's gastropubs seem set to inspire artists and musicians for years to come.

Intriguingly, and at vague risk of turning *The Seldom Seen Kid* into a concept album, the same character inhabits 'The Bones Of You', albeit in a younger guise. This person strides purposefully through St Anne's Square in Manchester and just past the Royal Exchange he pauses, phone welded to ear. Smartly clad in loose Armani suit, brown brogues and a briefcase that would cost more than a three-year-old Astra, this yuppie is the epitome of the modern go-getter – the very person who always seems to be striding through St Anne's Square. Suddenly, a song emerges from the yellow and blue doorway of a cappuccino café and immediately transports him five years and 3,000 miles, straight back into the arms of a woman.

The point is this guy has fallen to the force of his own ambition and self-absorption – a quest that wrenched him from the arms of this love and set him on a journey into success but, at the same time, isolation. The theme is blatantly obvious and even poignant, arriving as it did with a recession imminent. The bigger picture of this intensely personal tale was the immense folly of the "greed is good" attitude, of yuppiedom, of the chino-clad characters filling up the pseudo-industrial flat-block balconies of regeneration Manchester. The message is simple – what you want isn't necessarily what you need.

Garvey fully admitted that there was an autobiographical element, his relationship with a girl that suffered as Elbow moved into ferocious ambition overdrive. One thinks back to Elbow performing at Manchester's tiny Academy Three, seemingly lost to the world of celebrity, pushing what seemed like a lost cause and, naturally, the strain that such a struggle must place on any relationship. Garvey is humble enough to realise that the very same pressures, if not more, might affect a travelling salesman. When in a band, the partner has to live the dream or fall by the wayside.

The title 'Mirrorball' suggests a meet at the downbeat disco, but it could be merely symbolic for old-fashioned, Seventies-style romance – a love song ... plain and simple. The song's central character is caught in the afterglow, leaving a girl at her flat, swirling into a glorious morning when nothing can go wrong – nothing can damage this new love. There is no mystery here, no ambiguity, and it's a pity that more artists don't have the courage to tread these well-worn paths.

Quite the contrast to 'Mirrorball', which has a heart of gold, 'Grounds For Divorce' was a heart cry for freedom – from a marriage or relationship or a situation of entrapment. Even Manchester, which is always close to Garvey's heart, annoys on occasions. Life crowds you in sometimes. Garvey would later admit that the song sprang from the immediate aftermath of a stressful situation, possibly after being dropped by Island Records. It is not a lasting emotion. Reality, sense and love would creep back in but 'Grounds For Divorce' is about the lonely man at the bar, holding back the tears, bending the barman's ear, wallowing in self-pity.

The song became a favourite in Elbow's live set and, somewhat strangely, also became a problem for Garvey, as he explained to *Q*:

"It's got a really Tom Waits-esque feel, the first line of that song, it reminds you of that sort of ridiculous barroom, twisted gentleman figure that Waits is quite fond of writing about in his work. It's a funny one, really, the genesis of that song; I had the lyrics written down – before I really knew what they meant – and I had the riff kicking around for a good 10 years, and it took that long for me to put the two of them together. The little loop right at the start is from the original recording of the jam that the riff came from; it's a little snapshot from an Elbow jam around one microphone, and we just kept the same tempo and the same vibe from that session. In terms of the lyrics… well, things weren't great round here, after my mate died, and I just wanted to get out, really…

"Out of music, out of Manchester, out of the relationship I was in. I just didn't want anything to do with anything. And I eventually came round from it, and I realised that I was going through a period of mourning for my friend. Around that time, we were messing around with an old blues jam, and I thought, 'I need to get something out of this experience, something good'. That's one of the best things about being a 'creative', I think, that you can take something awful, and twist it around and make it pretty positive."

'An Audience With The Pope' is light-hearted, verging on the flip-pant with not a great amount of depth. Ironically, the themes it deals with – religion and sex – are anything but light. Garvey did not resent his Catholic upbringing, which provided him with many happy childhood moments. However religion often throws up paradoxes, especially to teenagers, with hormones raging and feeling pangs of guilt. It was difficult to stand in a holy church thinking impure thoughts, although undoubtedly there isn't a church goer alive who hasn't suffered in such a way. Here we see a writer barely skimming the surface, allowing the music to move the song right along.

Unlike most modern bands, Elbow had roots stretching back into boyhood aspiration. 'Weather To Fly' captures the band in a state of embryonic camaraderie and is the only song that Garvey has written to date about the band although it is truly distanced by the passing of times. Back then, these boys were lost to an unlikely dream, a dream that nobody else believed, with an unshakable confidence that many would feel was unwarranted. Perhaps they had a case because, if the talent was there, it had yet to be backed by musicality. In the song the boys fight, deflated by the fact that they are not particularly striking, in terms of songwriting, musicianship or looks. Looking back, Garvey finds it hard to believe how far away from any glint of success the band really was. Prior knowledge of this would have killed their aspi-rations. The message, therefore, is simple: no matter how adrift, never give up.

A metaphorical song crafted from the image of modern Manchester regeneration, 'The Loneliness Of A Tower Crane Driver' casts an eye across the city skyline to the sight of crane, swinging to and fro. And up there, locked in the cabin, the highest-paid workers in the construction industry, lost, alone, in a state of marginal danger and adrift from the camaraderie of fellow workers. It's the ultimate existential artisan existence (although truck drivers attain similar states of solitude), a song about the loneliness of naked ambition; the crane operator being prepared to get up early and return home late.

The comparison with a singer-songwriter might also be made here and, as ever, thoughts of Bryan Glancy – a true crane driver if ever there was one, would form in the mind. Of course, and most obvious of all, the rather lazy nod back to Alan Sillitoe's *The Loneliness Of The Long Distance Runner* (or, even more eclectic, Robert M. Mirsig's *Zen And The Art Of Motorcycle Maintenance*). It's a song written by a man who has read Camus but desires something rather closer to home.

'The Fix' tells the story of two Northerners who fix a horse race and blow the winnings. Garvey had befriended Sheffield singer-songwriter Richard Hawley and the two had talked of performing a duet together, although few could seriously imagine such a thing. Garvey duly introduced Hawley to the rest of Elbow and a bond was instantly formed. Initially, Garvey and Hawley had decided to write a serious duet but the balance seemed awkward... angst versus melancholy. Both writers realised that this would be risky and opted for a somewhat light-hearted affair. The intention was a kind of Flanagan and Allen mix of farcical notions.

"Richard Hawley was nicknamed 'The Alien' by Steve Osbourne, another former producer of ours," said Garvey. "He once observed him staying completely in time with a click track after it had faded out on him. It was apparently completely unprecedented. Nobody can to that. But Richard is a very special musician. A very special writer. On this occasion, Steve just faded it up again later on and there was Richard, still completely in time with the metronome. This freaked Steve out in a big way, hence the nickname 'The Alien'. He said that Richard was 'unworldly' and there is something very odd about him.

"He is a lovely person and a curious person. In fact, the only person that I know that can eat an entire Black Forest gateau in two mouthfuls – and does! And he eats kebabs and all that shit and he never puts on any weight ... I suppose that's the Sheffield in him. He has a grit that is covered in glamour ... well, elegance. Even to 'The Fix' he brought a certain smoothness to it. It flavoured the entire album actually."

'Some Riot' is a simple, effective and achingly sad song about addiction; that awful moment when the addict pulls away from the people who love them. More an observation than a warning, the song actually mirrors Glancy's song 'Propping Up The Bar' and takes on the perspective of the hapless addict, particularly the problem that occurs in the second stage of alcoholism, as the imbiber actually grows an awareness that everyone is watching and this, in turn, increases their paranoiac state. Given this state of affairs, the very last thing the alcoholic wants is the attention of other people, even close friends. It is a self-isolation that grows into a downward spiral. The addiction need not be alcohol, it could even be something relatively innocuous, but the song is about addiction rather than the substance.

As already mentioned, 'One Day Like This' was the final song that Garvey wrote for the album and tells of a bright summer high with the band having gained their new contract with Fiction and all manner of possibilities opening up once more. It's a metaphorical second chance song, for Elbow had long since used up their quota of 'breaks'. By this time, most bands in a similar situation would have disintegrated, their dreams disassembled, and floated sadly back into normal existence. The realisation not only that they were to be given another crack but, as Elbow knew, that their best was yet to come, fuelled the joy within this song. There is a tentative parallel to be made with Van Morrison's wry 'Days Like These' where the singer can hardly believe how good life fleetingly feels. Similarly with 'One Day Like This', Garvey's very northern observation is that just one great day a year is enough to inspire hope. Elbow had been through the mire...this song is positive proof of that and couldn't have been written without that particular level of experience. The 'Hey Jude'-style finale powers the song to a logical and uplifting conclusion.

'Friend Of Ours' is a self-explanatory ode to Bryan Glancy and, beyond that, the humility that arrives whenever a close friend dies. The song is like a slap around the face – no matter how good things get, as in 'One Day Like This', it can all collapse in an instant. When illness seeps powerfully in, when you are face-to-face with death, then only at that point do you fully realise how extraordinary life is. At its most basic, this song is a celebration of the extraordinary

Glancy. However, it is also a kick-back song that offers Garvey a mirror towards his own existence and its increasing fragility.

In the face of this most existential realisation, all the traumas, fights and horrors of struggling in a band pale into insignificance. It doesn't matter, in the end, just how successful Elbow may become nor does it matter if manager Phil Chadwick is doing cartwheels en route home from his Runcorn office or that the bank manager is finally smiling. Sometimes none of this bullshit really matters. If Glancy had never picked up a guitar, he would still have been the amazing guy he was. People place such a lot of stock in what they do, rather than what they really are. Were Elbow heading for the Mercury Prize? Big deal.

Speaking to the *Guardian*, Garvey noted: "A lot of songs perpetuate the myth that all relationships are either on or off and feelings either black or white. But I think the best heartbreak songs are the ones that mix up feelings of loss and pride and self–denial with feelings of 'carry on' and 'get on there'. I have never written a heartbreak song about one specific person. There are always those familiar feelings that come up at those times. I may be moved by my circumstances – through losing a friend or splitting up with someone- to write that kind of song, but I will be drawing on that familiar place where I have been before. Because I have been filling journals since I was 14 with my thoughts, I can go back at any point. Nostalgia always has an air of melancholy to it.

"The purest heartbreak song I've ever written is 'Friend Of Ours', which closes our last album, because that's the most heartbreak I have ever felt. Losing someone is a very difficult thing to bear and I am lucky that I get to turn it into something that hopefully comforts other people. That's one of the great things about having any sort of creative life. You can take those feelings and turn them round by writing a song about them."

For the first time in their career, the band really knew that they had made a truly special record.

"Craig's [Potter] done us really proud on this record," Garvey told the *Guardian*. "He's messed with stereo in a way that very few people are doing these days – not total separation, just giving things their own space. We really wanted to get a bit more experimental again on this album; for example, my favourite-sounding song on the current album – also my favourite personal song – is 'Weather To Fly'. The rhythm track there is made up of piano sounds; not keys, though, but us hitting the body of the piano and slapping the lid. [Craig Potter's] a clever bastard, he is; you know, that's another reason that we're together after all this time. I'm prone to exaggeration, but the rest of the band are all individually the most capable and skilled musicians at their instruments that I've ever come across."

The Seldom Seen Kid was another excellent Elbow effort, gaining widespread critical plaudits – it would be the fourth time the band gained a 9/10 rating in the *NME* – but this time, the band would not remain confined to the shadows. The possibilities were immense and, for once, Elbow were breaking out of any trace of false modesty. A headstrong Garvey even marched into Universal's boardroom to openly address the marketing team who would be working on *The Seldom Seen Kid*. Garvey told them that Elbow would help in any way they could with regard to promotion. "Because this is really gonna work," he asserted and, for once, this corporate-like commercial pre-monition carried considerable weight.

Chapter Eleven

Reluctant Heroes

Craig Potter acknowledged Elbow's new-found and rather unlikely confidence when he told Chris Salmon of the *Guardian*: "I think that as soon as we had finished [*The Seldom Seen Kid*] we knew that we had a very special album."

Elbow had never quite felt that way before although they had certainly taken on board the promotional failure of *Leaders Of The Free World,* which they had 'lost' due to cutbacks at V2. Whereas the band had to largely abandon the promotion of *Leaders* because they had completely lost faith in the record company, this time Fiction's healthy position meant that they could match and back up the band's success blow-for-blow.

Craig Potter: "We did change some of the songs in a way that wouldn't normally happen. But it wasn't a problem. We actually used a program called ProTools, which more or less bookmarks where you are in a song so ... well what happens is that, you can go back, so you're able to reference where the song was going. It's precious too because musicians can often take a song totally down the wrong path. Everyone does that and we are no exception. It's the cause of so much studio angst and has always been one of the major problems of being in a studio. That's why it's sometimes better to record almost live.

"But ProTools means that we can go too far and it's not a problem because there is no way you can record yourself into a corner. We find it's better to go too far so you can bring yourself back than to not know what can happen, what's possible. We've always been aware of that when we're working by ourselves, but I think we've got a good balance in this band. We all pitch in. We are all pretty democratic really and it works; the only time when I think you could say the record suffered a bit from over-embellishment was on *Cast Of Thousands*."

Craig Potter: "*The Seldom Seen Kid* is a much more personal album than *Leaders Of The Free World*. I think the rest of the band would agree with me on that. I've done a few interviews about it and Guy has done hundreds, it seems, and it has dawned on us, while talking about it, just how different the two albums are. I don't think we realised this at the time. But it is a natural ongoing process. Every album we have done kind of documents the time since the previous record. Thinking back, the title of *Leaders* was definitely saying something, but this is a much more personal record because of the way it was recorded too.

"*Leaders* was done in a big room in Blueprint Studios, the size of a five-a-side football pitch. *The Seldom Seen Kid*, by contrast, was recorded in like a decent-sized bedroom really, so we were all shut away at the top of this studio and I think you can feel that in the record. It has a closer, more intimate feel whereas *Leaders* [was] more on the big noise, anthemic side. Even the sprawling songs such as 'One Day Like This' have a certain intimacy about them."

When Joy Division recorded their second album, *Closer*, at Britannia Row Studios in London, producer Martin Hannett concentrated on getting so close to the Curtis voice that the result would add an unusual and poignant intimacy; the voice is gentle, closer to the ear. A similar effect not only highlights the difference between the last two Elbow albums, it would also be a major factor in the success of the new record. The Garvey voice, beyond all else, is warmer, friendlier and closer on *The Seldom Seen Kid* than on any of the previous Elbow albums.

Craig Potter: "The writing process is always quite democratic with Elbow. It always has been. There are five of us and we all value each others' opinions. If we can't agree on something it tends to go to the vote, but the times when you fall on the wrong side of the general consensus you just have to think, 'I trust these guys, and there's a reason they think the way they do'. We have slowly built this up over the years. It's a trust thing. That said, I do think that Guy is very much the focal point of *The Seldom Seen Kid*."

The Seldom Seen Kid also caused another silent phenomenon during the course of 2008. It may well have been to the artist's own discomfort, but the omnipresence of Guy Garvey in broadsheets and those monthly music glossies devoured by greying middle-aged (and somewhat sad) males such as this writer. People who, having experienced much of the world and having decided that they don't really have the inclination to experience much more of it, decided to take refuge in the arms of an old friend. Music and all its comforting nuances, from the Sixties onwards, through the shards of punk, the relaxed intelligence of post-punk, the bright blast of Eighties pop and the rock resurgence of the Noughties. In Elbow they got the band they always wanted; a band with shades of each era and, in Garvey, something more.

He could be seen as a man's man, slightly shabby, overweight, beery and intelligent. Males of a certain age enjoy the notion that such a person could become a rock star. They enjoy the fact, also, that the world appears to want to listen to what he has to say. Briefly, Garvey was stupidly called Mr Manchester. He was uncomfortable with this — embarrassed too. He never wanted to be thought of in such a way. "Tony Wilson was the only Mr Manchester," he would state emphatically.

Nevertheless Garvey has grown comfortable with his appearance of anti-glamour. Far from being a putdown, this is a trick that has taken a tremendous amount of charm and a little courage. There is a twist though. Guy Garvey may not be Mel Gibson or even Russell

Crowe (who, himself, has evolved into Hollywood's favourite anti-glam persona) but he has – I am reliably informed – become sexy in his own right. This might be down to simple charm and intelligence, but one senses more for Garvey has emerged from a central Lancashire that, still in many areas, clings fondly to the idea that its finest men are, in the lyrics of a song by Fivepenny Piece*, "A straightforward Lancashire lad".

The song celebrates (rather than satirises) the stereotypical notion of a Lancashire lad being beery, insensitive, prone to violence on any given Saturday and with not an awful lot happening between the ears.

While, at first glance, Garvey might appear like such a person – and, believe me, they do still exist – thanks to his curiously feminine lyrical vision, shot through with colour, romance and feminine sensitivity, more easily compared with Bat For Lashes or Kate Bush. Not since Morrissey – who noticeably back-tracked in the Nineties – has such a figure emerged. Garvey was beginning to challenge all these deeply ingrained preconceptions and, for men similarly adrift at the edge of middle age, it was rather liberating. How such a man could fold his heartbreaks, bitterness, hopes and love into such lyrics was almost a new find altogether … especially by a man from Bury.

June 14, 2008: One of the most curious venues in the north of England and undoubtedly one of the most beautiful. Approaching the natural bowl of a venue at Delamere Forest, in the heart of Cheshire, is almost unique for as you slide down the idyllic Cheshire lanes, past black'n'white-beamed pubs, through picture postcard villages, down long tree-lined avenues whether approaching from Warrington in the north or Staffordshire to the south, it is impossible to escape the soothing gentleness of the landscape built from the industrial revolution. This is the soft underbelly of Manchester (and Liverpool) and tension evaporates away with every breath.

---

* Fivepenny Piece were a hugely successful Seventies folk ensemble from Ashton-Under-Lyne who specialised in Lancashire history, folklore and the exaggerated cliché.

Even turning into the venue's makeshift car park fails to break this surreal vision. Then comes the steady traipse through two long fields, around the rim of the bowl. We came, also, for the myriad delights of UB40 (who largely attracted a crowd of over 50s bringing an unexpected edge to the gig), and local lads The Charlatans (revved-up thirty somethings) while the Elbow crowd seemed completely beyond age, genre or sartorial description.

Soothed by beer and the tinge of mud and grass, we soaked in the festival spirit by watching an ever precocious set from I Am Kloot. The perfect Elbow support, one might suggest, although, on artistic terms, very much an equal joy. Then came Elbow themselves, warping into the warm air, feeling quintessentially English, smiling into the breeze, joyful brass as the sun broke through and the crowd, fuelled on burgers and hummus, beer and little bottles of wine, gathered to form a large semi-circle of appreciation and the music drifted around the treetops, melting into the undulating Cheshire hillocks.

It was quite impossible to taste the sheer charm of the event and, in particular, of this band. Ironically in a landscape quite the antithesis of their Lancashire home, just 40 miles away, in a harsher landscape. I swear that the landscape teased a folkish evocation from those lovely lilting guitars, not exactly Fairport's Cropredy but, strangely, not so far adrift. Not far at all. After the event, and after much in-car queuing, the crowd disappeared into the Cheshire blackness. Perfect.

If one song became the anthem of the drizzly British summer of 2008, it was undoubtedly 'One Day Like This'. Synched into everyday lives via copious television usage on the Olympic Games and a scattering of football games and documentaries as well as sneaking into TV links and credits, with its beautiful refrain, soaring strings and vocals, 'One Day Like This' seemed to add irony and melancholy to endless days of greyness.

"It's looking like a beautiful day ..." would swill around the heads of new lovers and festival goers as they attempted to make the best of it, either stuck in the mud at Hylands Park or at the mighty Glastonbury.

Guy Garvey: "The biggest downside to a festival is that you can't ever get a proper soundcheck, you just gotta get on and play. You've got to rely on the speed and efficiency of your crew, and the local crew as well. Playing without a soundcheck can be utterly nerve-racking; you really are flung into the deep end with an audience watching. The big plus to playing a festival is... there's no soundcheck! Because I do find them boring. So, swings and roundabouts, really. I also love the fact that you have a floating crowd at festivals, not everybody's there specifically to see you, and you can see these people and whether or not they're getting into it. That's always interesting."

Elbow were certainly one of the highlights of the 2008 Glastonbury festival. To the band's delight, their stunning performance (with pre-taped brass) and Guy Garvey's big heart touched the astonishing vastness of the audience languishing in the Somerset mud. In truth, top slot on the main stage might have been even more indicative of their enormity. The set took place in the twilight slot on the second stage, just as the rarely glimpsed sun was setting to provide a suitably evocative backdrop. The crowd packed the second-stage field to capacity and, if health and safety hadn't been so steadfast, it would have swelled dangerously.

Elbow seized the moment and few could have walked away into the night, back to their tents, without 'One Day Like This' swirling around their heads. It would prove a galvanising moment; whenever the song might appear unexpectedly from a nearby radio or television, it would transport the festival goer straight back to that muddy field. With respect, for they are all good bands, it's difficult to imagine The View, The Enemy, Editors or Interpol enjoying this kind of immortality. This is because Elbow are not providing a blast on some distant field, they are submerging into people's lives.

After the Glastonbury and Latitude festivals, Elbow's fan base exploded overnight. Speaking to the *Guardian* in September 2008, Craig Potter noted: "That's where we really noticed that things were stepping up. For the last few albums, we would look out at festival crowds before we were due to go on and there would be nobody there. People would usually only turn up once we started playing. But it's not really been like that this time. . They have all been there, waiting for us to come on."

Mark Potter: "We have felt elated after every show whereas, previously, it had been something of a struggle. In a sense it has been much easier for us ... so much easier to play before an audience who are really behind you and know all the songs. There is nothing to prove and you can relax a bit. It seems more natural and it has certainly been more fun this summer than ever before."

The summer was full of other dizzying highlights. At Massive Attack's Meltdown Festival at the Royal Festival Hall the band used a 40-piece-male voice choir to full effect. Garvey once recalled how the eerie power generated by the Welsh rugby crowd had seemed so spiritually moving. That such a beautifully dour sound might shadow Elbow's music hardly requires a great leap for the imagination. However this was further augmented by the band being granted permission to make use of the Festival Hall's gargantuan pipe organ.

"Playing the songs live is quite good fun," Garvey said, backstage at Suffolk's Latitude Festival. "It's a big challenge to us. I have said this a few times but you do forget songs, no matter how much you rehearse and, when you go out live you are never quite sure that you can really play them. I am always amazed by people like Mark E. Smith who can change band members and yet still instil the ethos of the band within them. How does that work? They always sound edgy and perfect ... well perfect for them. When we play live we are occasionally out of our comfort zone and that's a scary place to be. It dawned on me that Mark Smith lives outside that zone. The Fall are always outside it and they wouldn't be The Fall if they weren't. We are not like that. But we do like to play around a little bit and try things out. But just trying to think back to how we recorded the songs is difficult enough, never mind putting a different spin on them every time we play live.

"Yes, often you can't remember what you were actually doing when you recorded a track; it just seems like such a long time ago. At the moment Craig is trying to work out the piano part to 'Mirrorball'. Now I wrote it with him, and the last time he tried to play it, it was totally divorced from what it sounds like on record. So he's rehearsing it over and over again."

Craig Potter: "We never really try to write a hit … whatever that is. We always try and find a balance, really. If we keep doing this we need to have some measure of commercial success, but we try and balance it. We certainly wouldn't want to compromise a song just to get it on the radio. That's something we've always felt very strongly about and something we'll always come up against. I mean a fourth album for a band that sells what we do – I mean if we go gold, that's a lot of records to me, but for some bands that would be a disaster. We always say we kind of fly under the radar and we see a steady rise every time we put something out. That's why after putting four albums out that haven't sold massive amounts, we still manage to be quite important in the grand scheme of things. I think that's quite a nice way of doing things – like bands like Pulp who took a long time to get there, but people are always interested and they never lose column inches, so I think we're in an enviable situation really."

Chapter Twelve

Mercury Rising

Actually, Elbow winning the Nationwide Mercury Prize on 9 September, 2008 *was* a big deal, the biggest deal of any Mercury Prize because it bypassed the patronising nature of the most eclectic artists and managed to overlook, too, the most obviously popular winners. But there was a crucial difference: everybody knew that Elbow should win.

Commercially speaking, as with the Booker Prize, winning the Mercury would provide a surge of retail electricity, an immediate shot to the tills. For immediately prior to the ceremony and following a string of high-profile festival gigs, *The Seldom Seen Kid* racked up more than 100,000 sales, enough to fire a debutant band into the most immediate headlines but not quite enough to secure a future for Elbow who were, by and large, drinking in the last-chance saloon.

Once past the Mercury glories however, the album immediately sold a further 130,000 copies, enough to seriously guarantee the band's future and push beyond expectations for an album that, as great as it was, would sit in the shadows of other major-selling outings from acts such as Kings of Leon, The Killers, and Oasis.

Garvey's unqualified support of the Mercury Prize probably had its roots in Badly Drawn Boy's win, back in 2000, in which the young Damon Gough had been most magnanimous, openly stating that it "belonged to all of Manchester". However, Garvey also believed that the Mercury Prize was the complete antithesis of *The X Factor*, which he hated, telling the *Guardian*, "I find the auditions for *The X Factor* cruel and heartbreaking. Those are people's daughters, mothers, sisters and wives and they are being fucking humiliated and Simon Cowell makes a fortune out of feeding people that shit."

By comparison, the Mercury was and is a celebration of people who have made a worthwhile record for nothing other than a love of music. Its raison d'être was based on something positive, spotlighting music that people might not normally hear; the promotion of eclecticism on a mainstream level. Nothing could be further removed from *The X Factor*.

During Elbow's acceptance speech, Garvey said, "Thank you very much. I'd like to thank all the players we've been with since day one, including Phil Chadwick, our manager. This is the best thing that's ever happened to us. We'd like to dedicate this award to Bryan Glancy, one of the greatest men who ever lived. Thank you very much and have a top evening!"

Elbow had been up against stiff competition from a variety of artists including Radiohead, British Sea Power, Laura Marling and the book-ies' favourite, Burial. Garvey later expressed his surprise at the band's victory, saying, "I had a tenner on Radiohead. It just feels great, very unexpected. You look at it in the same way as Bedouin tribes look at a pint of milk. It doesn't happen very often but it's all the sweeter. It's been a long time we've been doing it so it's cause for celebration. To the rest of the lads I'm so proud to do it with it with my best mates."

"We deserve a few days of getting absolutely twatted," Garvey exclaimed to the *Guardian*, the day after the awards. "I was so pissed last night my right eye didn't work when I woke up this morning."

Rarely do people speak to such an august journal in such a way. Even Mark E. Smith, in the throes of inebriation, would never pub-licly admit to something as unfashionable as binge drinking. But the band deserved it and Elbow fans and *Guardian* readers alike – for increasingly they had become the same beast – deserved a bit of old-fashioned Northern honesty.

No one could blame them and it seems that Manchester was universally proud. It was difficult to imagine such civic pride in. say, Oasis or The Smiths. There was something different going on with Elbow and the Mercury success simply highlighted this fact. With the Mercury Prize winners hogging each and every headline, the Elbow boys entered into a few days of becoming "twatted", heading for the nearest available, and somewhat downbeat, pub. Once there the simple, unaffected and equal banter between band and locals was not unlike an evening with Ricky Hatton in Hyde's New Inn. The talk was excitable with tales of the band members receiving standing ovations in London's many after-hours drinking holes they'd visited the previous evening.

Their mobile phones were overflowing with congratulatory text messages. Ex-Smiths bass player Andy Rourke fired a text succinctly stating: "Manchester is proud of you."

The entire band agreed on one point. This was the pinnacle, thus far, of their achievement and that fact had been rammed home by the flood of celebration in their home city. One friend telephoned to state that, upon hearing of their victory, he'd jumped up and down and broken his sofa. This had Garvey in tears. His old flatmate sent a text stating: "You lot are better at music than Stephen Hawking is at science." What read like a daft statement was enough to instil an even greater sense of pride.

In a beautiful gesture, Elbow decided to give their Mercury trophy to Bryan Glancy's mother. In the months following the win, Glancy would feature in a number of newspaper eulogies, which – *Manchester Evening News* aside – always eluded him while he was alive. It was also good to see his name becoming accessible by Google and his songs finally getting through to people.[*] Garvey put Glancy's obscurity

---

[*] It reminded this writer of the time Glancy won the Piccadilly Radio Busker of the Year competition. I recall the look of concern on his face when he realised that his songs would be played every morning on the Tim Grundy Show – it was a flash of panic, rather than pride.

down to a bipolar disorder. While that is certainly true, singer-song-writers such as Glancy had no way of breaking through at that time and it is *still* incredibly difficult, as the music business demands more in terms of image than the lonesome troubadour. Hopefully Glancy will now receive his proper due. I know he would have been so pleased if that were to be the case.

The success of Elbow as local heroes was fully commemorated by two sell-out Manchester 'homecoming' gigs in October 2008 at the Apollo in Ardwick. It did not go unnoticed by the band that this splendid theatre held a deep and lasting legacy as a legendary music venue within the city. From the extraordinary scenes of destruction at the 1978 Clash-Richard Hell tour to the two-night pairing of Buzzcocks and Joy Division a year later, from Iggy Pop's twin appearances in 1977 — one with David Bowie famously understated on keyboards — to Bruce Springsteen, Bob Dylan, Kraftwerk … it was easy to name a hundred classic Apollo gigs. The aging one time picture house always held a special atmosphere, a unique intensity that refused to fade even with the latter-day practice of stripping out the seats from the stalls to increase the venue's capacity.

Elbow's twin peaks of 2008 would equal just about anything that echoed through those dusty hallowed halls in the previous three decades.

Before the first show, Garvey was interviewed in the BBC's makeshift studio for Andrew Marr's Sunday morning show — an exposure not granted to every upbeat pop star gaining column inches in the broadsheets.

"Manchester looks beautiful today," quipped Marr, as shards of sunlight burst through Deansgate.

"Manchester is beautiful when it rains," Garvey replied, even if his demeanour appeared rather uncomfortable. He seemed happier meeting journalists immediately prior to the two gigs, confirming, "Manchester gigs are always different from anything else we do".

On 23 October, things certainly seemed different. Crowds swirled through Ardwick, cars filtered into makeshift car parks, and touts were heavy with anticipation; shout, rants and deals in the dark.

As the house lights dimmed, Guy Garvey came onstage to introduce support act singer-songwriter Jessica Hoop. Garvey pleaded to the home crowd to give her a chance as she was special and there at the band's request. However without her band, she appeared slightly lost, tentative. Most of the punters departed to the bar, downing quick fire pints and that third bottle of wine at inflated prices. When Garvey reappeared to perform a duet, the ripples of applause widened. It was not something normally applauded by managers and promoters – for the main act to appear with the support traditionally dilutes the mystique of the headline act. Garvey knows this but didn't care. This was Manchester and they could listen – they *would* listen.

The future is full of promise for Elbow and in Guy Garvey, the music world has at last found the perfect anti-star. They are not to everyone's taste. Those that like their rock or pop to be well dressed, exacting the perfect sellable image, do sometimes struggle with Elbow.

"Elbow? The world's most boring band," opines a music-loving friend of mine. As her favourite band might be CSS, it's easy to conclude that Elbow are a male phenomenon. However this writer begs to differ. There is an inherent femininity within Garvey's lyrics that helps explain why, when selecting their 'Festive Fifty' best songs of 2008, the diligent readers of *Word* magazine, with "a voice of ringing clarity" chose six tracks from *The Seldom Seen Kid*. Number one on the list was 'One Day Like This', with 'Grounds For Divorce' reaching number five. If nothing else, the list revealed Elbow's contemporaries to be the likes of Fleet Foxes, MGMT, Goldfrapp, Sigur Ros, The Hold Steady and Vampire Weekend.

It was no coincidence that the majority of these bands enjoyed full-scale festival performances during 2008, sizeable pop festivals now proving the perfect way to launch eclectic music, especially as much of it downloads and splinters across the world.

Elbow continued their line of filmic success when 'Grounds for Divorce' was chosen to feature on the trailer for the highly rated Coen Brothers film *Burn After Reading*, starring Brad Pitt, George Clooney and John Malkovich. This was a significant step forward and towards the end of 2008, Phil Chadwick's office was full of prospective film tie-ins with deals large and small. It now seemed that any film wishing to gain that extra critical push would benefit from an association with this most beguiling of English bands. Elbow could be relied upon to add gravitas, familiarity and warmth to a soundtrack, Garvey's vocals, in particular, attaining an instantly identifiable aspect. The business was now building significantly on its own and Elbow's management's responsibilities had switched from battling to gain work and exposure, to battling against the oncoming tide of both.

Garvey and Potter ventured back into Stockport's Moolah Rouge Studios to produce the new I Am Kloot album on the two bands' joint-owned Skinny Dog Records.

"We have complete freedom, so it works superbly well," said John Bramwell. "Also, Guy and Craig are two people who really understand exactly what Kloot are trying to do. The thing is that we are a band of varying styles… more so than Elbow, although there are similarities. But whereas big record companies are unable to handle a band who produce music in differing styles, different genres even, Elbow have no problem with this. Why should they? It's not that difficult, really. We are a band who think out of the box. So are they. Mostly, artists are just not allowed to do that because it doesn't make commercial sense."

Garvey's wisdom, in particular, stretched through Moolah Rouge adding rawness to, in particular, 'Take Me To The Brink', a heady little song about the pleasures of a lock-in at a local pub and the dark thrills that might follow.

During February 2009, Elbow became Britain's 'red button' band, the talk of television remote huggers across Britain. At the touch of a button one could be united with rolling concert footage of Elbow performing the by now familiar *Seldom Seen Kid* expanded to super-lush dimensions by a 56-piece orchestra and choir. This brilliantly orchestrated idea came via a hugely expensive gesture from the record company, Fiction, and the Radio 2 bods who had started to claim the band as their own.

The event was all the more prestigious thanks to the venue, Abbey Road's Studio One – another factor that helped link the band with an older, wider audience.* It was certainly an indication of just how far the band had travelled. A year before, such an occasion would have seemed wholly ludicrous not to mention somewhat risky. Ever since Deep Purple's *Concerto For Group And Orchestra*, the very notion of marrying a rock band with classical instrumentation signified a spiral into prog-rock pomposity or at least, an indication of a band taking themselves far too seriously. One could imagine the Elbow juggernaut of the future carting such a gigantic beast from stadium to stadium rather in the overblown manner of a mid-Seventies Emerson, Lake and Palmer foray. Hopefully Elbow are far too intelligent to fall into such over-indulgence, although it's happened many times before and is something they need to be aware of.

On a similar note of warning, the band has now arrived at the gates marked stadium rock. This means that concerts will have to be large-scale productions and intimate performances will be saved for 'one-off' occasions. Not every band is comfortable at this stage. One could never imagine Joy Division, for example, performing in such arenas even if, to the angst of Ian Curtis, they were beginning to edge towards that particular place. By contrast, U2, REM and Coldplay are all bands seemingly built for such occasions. But what of Elbow? Where do they fit in the spectrum that runs from intimate small clubs to gargantuan stadiums? It's an intriguing question and one that the band will find the answer to for themselves.

Elbow appear to have ridden their changes in fortune with consummate ease. "I can't believe what I am doing today. It's fucking ridiculous," said Garvey, laughing. "Fucking ridiculous" or not, Elbow became accessible to a whole new audience of ageing trendies and notions of a band now climbing towards Coldplay middle-ground

---

* I cannot recall another act who would take 18 years to spread like wildfire. During this period no fewer than six London-based acquaintances called the author of this book to enquire, "Which Elbow record should I buy?"

status proved both encouraging and, to the die-hard fan who had followed them from the beginning, rather worrying.

Guy Garvey: "I've known Chris [Martin] for years. Our first dry
run, as it were, with Island Records before we got signed was during
the time that they got signed. We got the same lawyer, etc, etc. So I
met Chris after a gig of ours at the Camden Monarch when our first
EP came out. And I've met him several times since. And he's a lovely
bloke. I mean his world has completely changed because of his success. But I think the way he's handled it is brilliant. Yeah, he's a
respectful bloke. He tries to do something good with the power that
he's got. And if photographs with me and my girlfriend were worth
10 grand, I don't know what I'd do! But he's a lovely bloke."

Is this the 'softening' process in action? Could Elbow slide to a natural blandness as so many had before? Even *The Seldom Seen Kid* is, to
many long-term Elbow aficionados, a step back from the edge. The
questions will probably be answered with the arrival of Elbow's fifth
album – the first time the band will be writing for a mainstream audience.

An eye to the future may lie in the one band who all five members
of Elbow agree on: Radiohead. Arguably no other British band has so
successfully pulled back into areas of often stunning experimentalism
while maintaining their upward trajectory. This became most obvious
on their celebrated 2007 release, *In Rainbows*, arguably their finest
outing since *OK Computer* a full decade earlier. Speaking in the May
2009 issue of *Clash* magazine, Garvey hinted that Radiohead's intelligent approach might provide the most profound influence on the
future of Elbow.

"It's funny, with a band as prolific as they are you're expecting mir-
acles every time they release a record. This one [*In Rainbows*] took a
little time to grow into everybody's hearts because they challenge
you, that's what they do. They don't give you what you want, they
give you what you need. My first listen was after I had downloaded it
and it was just kind of a once-through. I think I was pondering it
more than I was enjoying it. It's difficult sometimes – we were in the
middle of writing something at the time. When that's the case, I can't

listen to contemporary music without analysing it. I have to listen to old stuff – jazz and things. Stuff that's only loosely related to what we do.

"You can tell that they [Radiohead] are friends, you can tell they really care for each other, you can tell that they love making music together and the music they make is astonishing, generous and big hearted. Even if they were indulging themselves, that's what they do. They make music. They are only gonna make music that they enjoy. By that rationale then, anyone who ever makes a record is self-indulgent. It's loving something, enjoying something."

As with Radiohead, the marriage of commercial and aesthetic innovation is the probable route for Elbow. More than that, Radiohead have proved that it can work. Ten years previously, Blur imploded after trying the same. Elbow are similarly balanced. What roots them, however, is the organic nature of their 18-year rise to prominence. They now know that they have to make themselves happy and success alone is not enough to achieve this. They have to trust the muse and hope it accords in sales.

Not easy but, should they remain on that track, they could join Radiohead as a band at the peak of their artistic powers while enjoying critical and commercial success. Now that's some place to be.

Chapter Thirteen

Beyond The Brits

The *Abbey Road* concert, which emerged on CD and DVD in April 2009, was a triumphant blend of media planning and artistic intent. The band walked into the room with a noticeably chuffed Garvey failing to suppress the childlike grin that returned several times during the performance. A choir, full orchestra and greater level of instrumentation coupled with the controlled environment of a quality studio actually suited *The Seldom Seen Kid*. In fact, the live recording surpasses the original album in this writer's view. This became immediately apparent during the addictive intro to 'Starlings', which, at Abbey Road, would see the violent horn blasts slightly muted, which is how they should have been on the album.

There were standout moments on the *Abbey Road* recording that weren't necessarily the same as the album. 'Grounds For Divorce' is, as expected, a great driving, clanging beast with Garvey almost bent double as he hurls his voice to the fore. 'The Fix' sees the welcome sight of Richard Hawley and proves suitably joyous. However, the true triumph is the further orchestration on 'One Day Like This', which simply enters a whole new arena. Particularly in the final 'pick up' where the choir kicks on and the repetitive, "Throw those curtains wide…" line. For the first time, the true power and possibility of Elbow becomes evident. This was no ordinary band and the *Abbey Road* recording exists as proof that this might be the finest Manchester band of all time.

There was a further coincidence regarding the success of the *Abbey Road* recording. It arrived at a time when, often in an unholy scramble, artists and bands were agreeing to stage whole performances of their 'classic albums'. Patti Smith's *Horses*, Lou Reed's *Berlin,* The Stooges' *Funhouse* and Echo And the Bunnymen's *Ocean Rain* were just a few examples of this retrospective treatment. It was also strongly the trend (in the case of Reed and the Bunnymen) to fully revive the orchestrated aspects of the original work. While the cynic might point to the commercial benefits of suitably reinventing a timeless classic, almost all of these affairs not only proved successful but often started to shift far more units than the original (which isn't saying much in the case of *Berlin*).

Elbow's *Abbey Road* set held all these attributes, already feeling like a lost classic. It was almost as if *The Seldom Seen Kid* had first emerged in, say, the Eighties to modest success, only to be revived and reappraised in 2009 by the original band. In an abstract sense, the band that had been ignored for so long truly deserved such a time-honoured reverence. Most people drawn towards the Abbey Road event would have had little knowledge of the band a year before. Yet the warm connection between band and audience, between album and audience and between album and band, seemed timeworn.

Eighteen years from Bury garage to Mercury Awards, winning Best British Band at The Brits on 18 February, 2009, another esteemed industry award, saw Elbow finally accepted by the mainstream. The award is traditionally given to artists who have spent the past year in the full glare of celebrity, which was partly the reason why the world, or those who gave a damn, had been confidently predicting a win for comeback kings Take That, a band whose unlikely resurgence seemed to touch the hearts even of those naturally allergic to the concept of a 'boy band'. Just a few months earlier the very idea of Elbow being part of this glittering pop party would have seemed utterly absurd.

While a Brit did not seem like the natural award for Elbow, the band decided to at least embrace the occasion, inviting wives and girlfriends to the event, something which – to their eternal regret – hadn't happened at the Mercury Prize. Elbow had a sneaking feeling that they might have grasped the Best Live Band slot. However, when that award went to Iron Maiden – another inexplicable twist and a suggestion that the Brits was beginning to broaden and accept artists on merit alone – Elbow were resigned to merely enjoying the occasion, slightly reining in their natural hedonistic bent.

The tabloid press, an empty-headed beast at the best of times, failed to hand out the much-deserved compliments to Elbow, a band who they obviously saw as being outside their domain. Two different 'red tops' noted that "Coldplay had been robbed", a somewhat pathetic angle intended to save the face of their resident pop 'experts'. Elbow saw it as a good thing that they were not about to be fully embraced by tabloid Britain. It's difficult to see how they would have fitted. Having stated that, there is still something about Elbow's music – that ingrained melancholia – that seems to link it with everyday events. 'One Day Like This' was even used as television background for the 20th anniversary of the Hillsborough football disaster and no hint of flippancy seemed evident.

Down in a windswept, bitingly cold and out-of-season Blackpool, gargantuan and elongated monster trucks belonging to Elbow's perverse touring express arrive at the side of the Empress Ballroom, an ornate Victorian music hall within the Winter Gardens. The venue's image is eternally linked with ballroom dancing and antiques fairs, but it also holds a place deep in the heart of Manchester music aficionados, not least because of the legendary appearance by The Stone Roses who, on August 12, 1989, attained their 'perfect pop moment' by inviting, or so it seemed, the whole of 'Madchester' to a day out at the seaside. A year later, James achieved a similar frisson and this was not lost on the Gallagher brothers who, in 1995, made sure Oasis played the venue that would always be seen as the ultimate music day out for Manchester and beyond.

Curiously, the venue didn't seem to sit so easily with the grandiose sound of Elbow, who, on 7 March, 2009, performed with an intensity that seeped into the intricately designed ceiling. As if a continuation of Elbow's two homecoming Manchester gigs, Blackpool was seen as a celebration of an amazing 18 months – and marked 18 years for Elbow as a band. The bulk of the set naturally comprised *The Seldom Seen Kid*, this time spliced with a few oldies in acknowledgement of the long-term nature of this particular crowd. The gig was a success rather than a triumph due to the nature of the venue but it didn't matter in the slightest. Just a pity that the band's long-term Manc devotees weren't heavy in attendance two days later, as Elbow took charge of an even more unlikely venue, the Theatre Clwyd in Llandudno. The day was equally biting weather-wise – windy and rain-swept – even if the elegance of the town contrasted deeply with the modernistic nature of the venue.

A purpose-built hall may lack the emotive resonance of an olde-time music hall, but it certainly coped far better in terms of basic acoustics. One of the downsides of seeing Elbow at festivals, for example, is the lack of depth that can be produced on an outdoor stage. For those wishing to wallow in the band's dense hi-fidelity a gig such as the Llandudno Theatre is infinitely preferable.

The seaside gigs preceded the band's largest concert to date, the Wembley Arena show of March 14. It was to be a curious affair and the unconventional 'lead in' gigs in Brighton, Blackpool and Llandudno seemed significant, as if Elbow's last dewy-eyed blast in the intimacy of small, parochial venues. Wembley Arena dawned, as they all dreamed that it would, as a stark reminder of what lay ahead: the simple vastness of future performance; the ease of transport; the trappings of stardom.

"It was a joy to play there although there was a touch of nerves … part of me didn't feel like I truly belonged on that stage, even though the set went down very well and I think we performed – er – OK," Garvey reflected. "But I don't know. There is part of us that thrived on the connection with the audience, with the idea that we were all in it together ... band and audience against the world."

Well it was certainly a long way from Manchester's Roadhouse or the Night & Day Café, where members of the crowd would trip over the stage as they wandered to the toilet. The glee in realising true success had arrived was tempered by the knowledge that it might not be so much fun any more.

As if to amplify these feelings, within days the band had swapped spring in the UK for the shimmering sunshine of Australia's golden autumn when they appeared on the V Festival bill alongside Snow Patrol, Duffy, Kaiser Chiefs and The Killers. In Australia, Killers aside, it was viewed as a new wave of major British bands with Elbow's surreal northern imagery seemingly at home in the Australian rays. The event would herald a year of frantic festival performances including, back in the UK, the twin V Festivals of Highlands Park in Chelmsford and Staffordshire's Weston Park.

In July 2009, a further peak was reached when the band were given the chance to perform two concerts as part of the Manchester Festival, accompanied by Manchester's legendary Hale Orchestra, in the city's prestigious Bridgewater Hall, having eclipsed the Free Trade Hall (now a four-star hotel) as the world-renowned 'home of the Hallé'.

The significance of this might be lost on those not schooled in Manchester history – that five Bury boys should be fronting the most prestigious musical body ever to emerge from Manchester and arguably the British Isles. The pairing with Elbow signified a gravitas for the Elbow boys that arguably lay beyond the grasp of any other band to emerge from the city. Not that that is prestige alone; no one could imagine The Stone Roses or The Fall performing in front of such a backing (although elements of the Hallé have infiltrated The Fall's transient ranks). It is also true that Elbow's music, more than any other Manchester band I can think of, benefits from a classical backing.

Nevertheless, it was a prestigious achievement for the Hallé Orchestra has remained one of the great orchestras of the world since its inception in 1857 when German-born Charles Hallé, a close friend of Chopin, came to Manchester to escape the revolutionary angst in Paris. His orchestra became the first professional symphony orchestra in Britain. The subsequent history of the Hallé is built into the very fabric of the city, and its leaders have included such legendary figures as Hans Richter, John Barbirolli and, in recent times, Kent Nagano and Mark Elder. The shift from the Free Trade Hall to the Bridgewater Hall, controversial in the first instance, has come to symbolise Manchester's astonishing regeneration.

If these were to be Elbow's last ever concerts, God forbid, their status would be eternally assured and the strains of 'One Day Like This' and 'Grounds For Divorce' might echo around the city's streets, dipping and swirling like the starlings that have, themselves, gained an unlikely iconic status.

The Hallé gigs sold out within hours. Speaking to the *Manchester Evening News*, Guy Garvey found it difficult to contain his fervour.

"They're bringing their skills to the table and we're honoured that they are playing some of our tunes. I can't stress enough, it's not about us backed by the Hallé, it's about a collaboration of [Mancunian composer] Joe Duddell's work and our work. He's interpreted a lot of our stuff and written a lot of new material to accompany our stuff. I'm a huge fan of classical music. I used to collect requiems, in particular the *in paradisum* from any requiem. When a composer decided to write their own requiem mass, they have to write their idea of paradise. So it has to be the most beautiful piece of music they've ever written. There are some amazing *in paradisums*. My favourite one is Duruflé's."

The idea for the shows was for the band to 'mingle' with the choir and orchestra rather than front the gig and subsequently use the orchestra to swell their ego – therefore Pete Turner will sit with the string section with Garvey standing near the choir. Fittingly, the loose theme of the performance would be the city of Manchester itself, with obvious choices such as 'Station Approach', slotting perfectly into place.

"I've written more love songs to this city than I have to any one girl," said Garvey. "There's one on every record, pretty much. We wanted to do something really special that's about Manchester's best parts — its strong sense of community, its vibrant spirit, its welcoming attitude to people from outside Manchester. I'm so proud that we've got the biggest international student body in Europe. I'm proud that every September so many people choose to make the city their home for a few years."

The Halle gigs might be seen as a diversion, an extravagance best viewed as another example of the sheer flexibility of Elbow's music. To emphasise this further, and as something of an antithesis, at the same time as the Bridgewater Hall dates were announced, a rather more traditional show was booked at the city's concrete shell, the M.E.N. Arena, for September, intended as the swansong of *The Seldom Seen Kid* set. The M.E.N, a soulless venue that recently hosted The Sex Pistols, Morrissey, Leonard Cohen and AC/DC, could be seen by Elbow as the welcoming doors to a life of stadium rock. One strongly senses that the rest of the world will surely follow. If nothing else, it brings home the significance of life-changing success.

"I've got to give consideration to things I never have had to consider before, involving going out in public," Guy Garvey told *Manchester Evening News* journalist Paul Taylor. "But, generally speaking, the people who like our music are lovely. The people who come up and say 'cheers' or 'nice one' are always really pleasant. I can't say that my life is the same but I like to think that I am the same person. I'm still making music with my best mates, still in love with the same girl, still living in the same town."

Chapter Fourteen

A Free Man In Bury

Winning the Mercury Prize might have seemed rather surreal, snatching a Brits award maybe less so. Performing in front of the Hallé Orchestra was simply preposterous. But an even greater, even more bizarre honour would be bestowed on the Elbow lads on May 11, 2009. Hard to envisage how the boys who performed clunky covers of Chuck Berry numbers in that dusty rehearsal room could one day be granted ... the Freedom of Bury.

It is a strange world and it's getting stranger. But who could say that Elbow hadn't deserved such an honour, having literally taken a vision gained in Bury and sold it across the globe? Alongside Bury film-maker Danny Boyle, whose *Slumdog Millionaire* had similarly broken the mould, and paralympian Zoe Robinson, Elbow were proudly photographed clutching their medals, like soldiers returning from front-line bravery.

"In some ways this is the highlight of our career so far," Garvey told the *Manchester Evening News*. "It's great to be home with Danny and Zoe. You go to some ceremonies and they are televised and the celebrities are there, but this is the real deal."

It is interesting to note the grace and humility displayed by the new Bury superstars — a possible reason for this latest and most unlikely honour. Why Elbow in Bury? Why not Echo and the Bunnymen in Liverpool? Why not give Mark E. Smith the freedom of Salford? The answer is obvious really and reflects the fact that Guy, Craig, Pete, Mark, and Richard really are tremendous ambassadors for their hometown... and for Manchester beyond.

Where to now, then? While Garvey continues to state that he would like to move to New York, he also reflects that both he and his partner, a *Manchester Evening News* journalist and would–be author, have deep family links within the area alongside his own oft-expressed love of the Manchester of modern regeneration and his love of the countryside.

In Bury, the small-town atmosphere is both cheering and claustro-phobic, making it difficult to wander through the town's precinct without endless good cheer. In New York, he could melt away and, for a man who needs that tug of real life, who needs to watch other people from the same level, the rarefied atmosphere of superstardom may not make such a prolific muse.

However, as of May 2009, several new Elbow songs have already been written, if not recorded to any level above initial demos. "I can tell you what I have been doing lyrically and that's looking back," Garvey said.

There is a caricature of a vision that sees Elbow lumbering towards their next album, gaining prizes and award nominations this way and that, the sweat from toil heavy in the air. Could there be a point where such awards become genuinely cumbersome? Or embarrass-ing, even, especially for five modest men — by all accounts — who emerged with such dignity. Still intact, it seems, even if, quite natu-rally, they are simply being tugged this way and that by each success, leaving Phil Chadwick to perfect the art of saying 'no'.

And of course, just when holding an embarrassment of honours, two more should come along. On Thursday, May 21, Elbow some-what predictably picked up two Ivor Novello Awards at London's Grosvenor House — the scene of their original (and unsuccessful) Mercury Award nomination in 2001. 'One Day Like This' captured the 'Best Song Musically and Lyrically' gong while 'Grounds For Divorce' picked up 'Best Contemporary Song'.

Garvey seemed to ooze the contentment of a Cheshire cat. "If nothing else ever happens to me in my whole life then these four boys have made the whole thing worth every single second," he glowed.

Elbow's fellow winners were an odd and disparate bunch, to say the least. The underrated and remarkable triumph of Salford's The Ting Tings in the Best Album category might have raised a few eyebrows but to see them standing alongside Elbow, Smokey Robinson, Vince Clarke and Duffy was positively surreal.

Inevitably, the evening crumbled into another evening of alcohol-fuelled banter. Where would it end?

Almost before the new batch of awards had been handed out, the *NME*, among other organs of note, had started to call time on Manchester's success stories, gently suggesting that the city had reached a previously unparalleled lull in grass-roots activities. Elsewhere, the notion that Elbow would be the last truly inspirational band to emerge from the apparently dying city was also mooted – a notion that chose to ignore visibly burgeoning acts such as Twisted Wheel, Exile Parade, Frazer King and many others.

It seemed quite fitting, therefore, on Saturday, June 6, to visit Elbow's spiritual home at Blueprint Studios, a place where their presence seemingly permeates every corner. Close to Manchester city centre, yet just pushed into the fringe of Salford on Queen Street, despite its stark blue and white studio anti-chic, this catacomb building remains hugely evocative of the industrial heritage of the twin cities.

Even more significantly, the evening's event existed as part of the embryonic Unconventional music conference, Salford's indie-inspired answer to Manchester's In The City. While that yearly affair obviously played a huge part in the stuttering early career of Elbow, it has, arguably, become rather too institutionalised in recent years. To fill the breach, a number of spirited smaller conferences have become evident, Salford, Liverpool and Sheffield among them.

Blueprint is not the most intimidating of studios. No neatly coiffured blonde sits stonily behind a pristine reception desk, immediately challenging the worth of any denimed oik who may linger, bearing a demo tape. It does not seem to offer an instant cloak of glamour, of sexy studio warmth, the sense of a gateway to a wholly glamorous world. In fact, it immediately reminds this writer of a newly opened Kwik Fit Euro and I don't mean this unkindly. If nothing else it reflects the down-to-earth humility of the band who have helped to make it famous – a stack of flight cases boldly bearing the name ELBOW as a reminder.

This particular evening saw a flurry of disparate and precocious acts, headed by I Am Kloot, all linked under the 'Unconventional' banner. Computer printouts guided the crowd up three flights of stairs and into an unexpected 'live music area' at the top of the building; an immediately evocative space (a former classroom?) beneath a huge apex ceiling, heavily reminiscent of Manchester's Boardwalk venue i.e. a pristine, contemporary performance room built within a stark industrial atmosphere. To the left, a bar. To the front, a stage.

"Do many gigs take place here," I asked naively?

"No it's Elbow's room," came the reply.

Elbow's success permeates the air and seems to settle gently on the audience, on the artists, on the new scene. There are venues across the city with a similar vibe but on this night one sensed a continuum, if not a baton being passed. It instantly transported this writer back to 1985, to a time that saw the initial emergence of The Stone Roses, Happy Mondays, James and the musicians and audience that would roll towards the Madchester explosion of 1989. Back then, as now, the air at small gigs such as this seemed energised, be it by the bands, fanzine writers, photographers, promoters, or producers. In other words, the very template that had eluded the less fortunate Elbow for so long. Yet on this night, and hopefully on many more, a decent-sized, endearingly polite audience saw a parade of embryonic talent. Tombots are three young lads of electronic bent, already turning heads in London and Oldham, idiosyncratic and reminiscent of early

Pulp and The Fall. Also, Sisters Of Transistors, helped along by 808 State's Graham Massey.

"Yeah it feels good again in Manchester," he stated. "I think Elbow's success has filtered down in so many ways. There is no doubt that bands such as these have been inspired."

Massey looked content. I had known him, 25 years earlier, as the heady protagonist of Factory's avant-garde, funk-experimental outfit Biting Tongues. Back then, he/they seemed lost, spinning in an endless vortex of gigs that lay off the radar. But beyond the radar is a rich seam where all true individualism lies. Of all bands, Elbow understand this; the main reason why their unseen hand guides such events as this – a gig in the shadows. Elbow will always be a band from the shadows.

In the summer of 2009, the annual Manchester Festival brought a series of events to the city centre. Had the concerts, from Lou Reed, Anthony and the Johnsons and Kraftwerk, brilliantly placed in the city's cycling velodrome, just occurred with no unifying notion of 'festival', no one would have noticed. However, and much to the amazement of the organisers, the event that sold out within ten minutes of online credit-card frenzy wasn't any of the above artists but 'An Audience With Guy Garvey', cleverly constructed and timed to perfection by Manchester DJ and writer Dave Haslam. In a year when you could take your dosage of Elbow in a variety of ways (orchestrated in plush surroundings or blasting out in a gargantuan concrete shell, in mud-splattered festival splendour or on live DVD) the chance to catch a word from the man at the centre of the vortex seemed particularly appealing.

But, on the other hand, how odd, if not utterly bizarre. After all, for so many years, Garvey remained the content, amiable, omnipresent anti-star where, even in his numerous 'locals', few people really bothered to engage him in sycophantic conversation. Now they clamour to hear this talented and aloof Bury lad chatting at the pinnacle event of a large arts festival.

Maybe he is Mr Manchester, after all.

Elbow Discography

Powder Blue (July 2001)
CD1: Powder Blue/Suffer/About Time (Acoustic) (VVR 501616-3)
CD2: Powder Blue/Red (Acoustic Lamacq Evening
Session)/Powder Blue (VVR 501616-8)
10″ coloured vinyl: Powder Blue – About Time (Acoustic)/Powder
Blue (Andy Votel Mix) (VVR 501616-0)

Newborn (October 2001)
CD1: Newborn (Album Version)/One Thing That Was Bothering
Me/None One (VVR 50617-3)
CD2: Newborn (Album Version)/Lucky With Disease/Press Your
Lips (Newborn) El Presidente Remix (VVR 50617-8)
12″: Newborn (Album Version)/Lucky With Disease/ Newborn
bitten by The Black Dog

Asleep In The Back (February 2002)
CD1: Asleep In The Back/Coming Second/Stumble (VVR
501870-3)
CD2: Asleep In The Back/Coming Second (Misery Lab
Remix)/Stumble (VVR 501870-8)

Ribcage (online only single) (May 2003)

Fallen Angel (August 2003)
CD1: Fallen Angel/Loss/Whisper Grass (VVR 502180-3)
CD2: Fallen Angel/Brave New Shave/Fallen Angel (Dncn's Broken
Elbow Dub) (VVR 502180-8)
DVD single: (VVR 802180-9)

Fugitive Motel (October 2003)
CD1: Fugitive Motel – Switching Off (Acoustic Version)/Ribcage
(Andy Cato Mix) (VVR 502182-3)
CD2: Fugitive Motel (RJD2 Mix)/Love Blown Down/Ribcage
(Kinobe Mix) (VVR 502182-8)
DVD single: (502182-9)

Elbow Remixes (November 2003)
Ribcage (Andy Cato mix)/Fugitive Motel (RJD2 mix)/Ribcage
(Kinobe Mix)
(VVR 502182-6)

Not A Job (February 2004)
CD1: Not A Job/Teardrop (VVR 502467-8)
CD2: Not A Job/Lay Down Your Cross/Live On My Mind/Not A
Job Video (Soup Collective Version) (VVR 5022467-3)
Fugitive Motel/Theme From Munroe Kelly (2004 version) (DVD
VVR- 5022467-8)

Grace Under Pressure (July 2004)
CD: Grace Under Pressure (Edit)/Switching Off (Album
Version)/Waving From Windows/Fugitive Motel (Acoustic from
Radio 2's Stuart Maconie session)/Grace Under Pressure (live from
Glastonbury)

Forget Myself (August 2005)
7": Forget Myself/McGreggor (VVR 503254-7)
CD1: Forget Myself/Strangeways To Holcombe Hill In Four
Minutes And Twenty Seconds/My Finger/Forget Myself (video)
(VVR 503254-3)
CD2: Forget Myself/The Good Day (VVR 503254-8)

Leaders Of The Free World (November 2005)
7": Leaders Of The Free World/Gentle As (VVR 503562-7)
CD1: Leaders Of The Free World/The Long War Shuffle (VVR
503562-3)
CD2: Leaders Of The Free World/Mexican Standoff (Spanish
Version)/The Drunken Engineer (VVR 503562-8)

Grounds For Divorce (released and deleted in the same week –
March 2008)
CD: Grounds For Divorce/Hotel Istanbul

7" 1: Grounds For Divorce/Our Little Boat
7" 2: Grounds For Divorce/A Regret

One Day Like This (June 2008)
CD: One Day Like This/ Lullaby
7" 1: One Day Like This/Every Bit The Little Girl
7" 2: One Day Like This/Li'l Pissed Charmin' Tune

The Bones Of You (September 2008)
Promo CD: The Bones Of You (radio edit) – 3:06
Digital download: The Bones Of You/The Bones Of You (live at Manchester Academy)

ALBUMS

Asleep In The Back (CD/LP VVR 101588-2) (May 2001)
Any Day Now/Red/Little Beast/Powder Blue/Bitten By The Tailfly/Newborn/Don't Mix Your Drinks/Presuming Ed (Rest Easy)/Coming Second/Can't Stop/Scattered Black And Whites (Reissued in Feb 2002 VVR 101901-2 with extra track: Asleep In The Back)

Cast Of Thousands CD/LP (VVR 102181-2-1) (August 2003)
Ribcage/Fallen Angel/Fugitive Motel/Snooks (Progress Report)/Switching Off/Not A Job/I've Got Your Number/Buttons And Zips/Crawling With Idiot/Grace Under Pressure/Flying Dream 143

Leaders Of The Free World (VVR 103255-2-1) (September 2005)
Station Approach/Picky Bugger/Forget Myself/The Stops/Leaders Of The Free World/An Imagined Affair/Mexican Standoff/The Everthere/My Very Best/ Great Expectations/ Puncture Repair

The Seldom Seen Kid (Fiction 1764098) (March 2008)
Starlings/The Bones Of You/Mirrorball/Grounds For Divorce/An

Audience With The Pope/Weather To Fly/The Loneliness Of A
Tower Crane Driver/The Fix/Some Riot/One Day Like
This/Friend Of Ours
UK bonus track on CD and download versions only: We're Away

The Seldom Seen Kid Live At Abbey Road (a limited edition
package exclusively available through the official Elbow website;
released March 2009)
CD & DVD track listing:
Starlings/The Bones Of You/Mirrorball/Grounds For Divorce/
An Audience With The Pope/Weather To Fly/The Loneliness Of A
Tower Crane Driver/The Fix/Some Riot/One Day Like
This/Friend Of Ours